San Diego
Mountain Bike Guide

SUNBELT NATURAL HISTORY GUIDES
"Adventures in the Cultural and Natural History of the Californias"
A Series Edited by Lowell Lindsay

SOUTHERN OVERLAND ROUTE
Lowell and Diana Lindsay (1985)

BICYCLING BAJA
Bonnie Wong (1988)

ADVENTURES WITH KIDS IN SAN DIEGO
Judy Botello (1991)

HISTORICAL SITE MARKERS—
  KERN COUNTY
Bill Hample (1991)
(Kern County Historical Society)

GEOLOGY OF ANZA-BORREGO:
  EDGE OF CREATION
Paul Remeika, Lowell Lindsay (1992)

MOUNTAIN BIKE GUIDE—SAN DIEGO
  REGION, 3rd ed.
Scott Bringe (1993)

DESERT LORE OF SOUTHERN CALIFORNIA
Choral Pepper (1994)

GEOLOGY OF SAN DIEGO COUNTY
Edited by Diane Burns (1996)
Frederick W. Bergen, Harold J. Clifford, Steven G. Spear

THE CAVE PAINTINGS OF BAJA CALIFORNIA,
  3rd ed.
Harry Crosby (1997)

SAN DIEGO MOUNTAIN BIKE GUIDE
Daniel Greenstadt (1998)

Also by these authors:

OUR HISTORIC DESERT
Diana Lindsay (1973)
(Copley Books)

TREASURE LEGENDS OF THE WEST
Choral Pepper (1994)
(Gibbs–Smith)

ANTIGUA CALIFORNIA
Harry Crosby (1994)
(University of New Mexico Press)

ANZA-BORREGO AND YUHA DESERT GUIDE,
  4th ed.
Lowell and Diana Lindsay (1998)
(Wilderness Press)

San Diego
Mountain Bike Guide

DANIEL GREENSTADT

SUNBELT PUBLICATIONS
San Diego, California

COVER DESIGN   Court Patton—Patton Brothers Design and Illustration
BOOK LAYOUT & DESIGN   Guy and Debby Tapper—October Publishing Services
MAPS AND PHOTOGRAPHS   Daniel Greenstadt unless otherwise noted

All inquiries should be directed to publisher:
Sunbelt Publications, Inc.
P.O. Box 191126
San Diego, CA 92159-1126
(619) 258-4911

01 00 99   5 4 3 2

"Sunbelt Natural History Guides"
A series edited by Lowell Lindsay

Library of Congress Cataloging-in-Publication Data
Greenstadt, Daniel, 1964–
    San Diego Mountain Bike Guide / written by Daniel Greenstadt; photographs
    by Daniel Greenstadt; map illustrations by Daniel Greenstadt.
    p.   cm. — (Sunbelt Natural History Guides)
    Includes bibliographical references and index.
    ISBN 0-932653-24-3
    First Edition 1998.
    1. All terrain cycling—California—San Diego Region—Guidebooks.
    2. Bicycle trails—California—San Diego Region—Guidebooks.
    3. San Diego Region (Calif.)—Guidebooks.   I. Title.   II. Series.
    GV1045.5.C22S255   1998
    917.94'980453–dc21   97-44536
                                                            CIP

Photo Credits
Greg Lambert: 18, 110, back cover

Field research was performed atop a rigid, Gecko Cycles "Y File It" and a Curtlo Cycles
"Mountaineer" equipped with an Action-Tec "Pro Shock."
Cover photo - Images Copyright © 1997 Photodisc, Inc.

for Theresa,
and mountain bike widows everywhere

CONTENTS

Foreword   ix

Acknowledgments   xi

Introduction   xiii

THE RIDES
COASTAL CANYONS AND FOOTHILLS

1 The Tri-Canyons   1
   1a Marian Bear Memorial Park (San Clemente Canyon)   2
   1b Rose Canyon Open Space Park   4
   1c Tecolote Canyon Natural Park   7

2 Los Penasquitos Canyon Preserve   8

3 Balboa Park–Florida Canyon   11

4 Mission Trails Regional Park   13
   4a Cowles Mountain   14
   4b Suycott Wash Loop   18
   4c North Fortuna Peak   20

5 Lake Hodges–San Dieguito River Park   22

**6 Sycamore Canyon Open Space Preserve/
   Goodan Ranch   26**

7 Lake Poway and Twin Peaks   29

8 Daley Ranch–Escondido   34

9 Elfin Forest   37

10 Sweetwater Reservoir   41

MOUNTAINS

11 Anderson Truck Trail   47

12 Laguna Mountains   50
   12a Big Laguna Trail   50
   12b Noble Canyon/Indian Creek Trail   53

12c Sheephead Mountain Road   57
12d Kitchen Creek/Thing Valley Loop   59

13 Cuyamaca Rancho State Park   61

13a Grand Loop   63
13b Oakzanita Peak   66
13c Boulder Creek Loop Deluxe   68

14 Lake Morena/Corral Canyon   72

15 Palomar Mountain   75

15a West Side–Nate Harrison Grade   77
15b East Side   78

16 Indian Flats   80

17 Los Coyotes Indian Reservation   83

TRANSITIONAL AND TRUE DESERT

18 McCain Valley   89

19 Jacumba Mountains   90

19a Table Mountain   92
19b Valley of the Moon   95

20 Anza Borrego Desert   96

20a Three Canyons—Rodriguez/Oriflamme/Charriot   98
20b Grapevine Canyon   99

Appendix   102

Recommended Reading   105

Index   107

FOREWORD

For locals or first time visitors, there are few things as handy as a good guide-book. The San Diego Mountain Bike Guide, written by someone as knowledge-able about trails in the San Diego region as Daniel Greenstadt, is one of the best. Dan's work with the San Diego Mountain Biking Association, the San Diego County Trails Council and the International Mountain Bicycling Association puts him in a unique position to share his passion for trail riding.

Daniel shows the reader that coast to inland, the San Diego region offers trails with a wide variety of terrains, climates, and natural features. He whets our appetites for exploring San Diego's magnificent backcountry. On a given day, you can find freezing snow in the mountains or blistering heat in the desert. Coastal canyons are cooled by sea breezes. Close-in trailheads allow easy access from many neighborhoods, but there are harder-to-find trailheads too. San Diego County's greatest treasures are in this book, and we're told what to expect, how to prepare, and what not to miss.

Whether you're an experienced rider or you just bought your first mountain bike, there are trails in here for you to explore and enjoy. The sense of freedom that we get as we pedal through beautiful country never goes away. New trails are full of discovery, and trips on familiar routes almost always show us something new. Cycling nourishes our bodies, our minds, and our spirits. This book is a feast to which we've all been invited.

San Diego is one of those rare trail communities where mountain bikers, hikers, and equestrians are working closely together to acquire trail linkages and to pre-serve open space. As you enjoy these rides, remember that, as part of the trail community, we have responsibilities to ride gently, to expect and respect one another, and to contribute the sweat equity to keep these and new trails open forever.

Jim Hasenauer
Director of Education,
International Mountain Bicycling Association

ACKNOWLEDGMENTS

This guidebook is the shared creation of many people and I would like to thank just a few of the individuals and organizations whose assistance and guidance I gratefully acknowledge. Without them I'd still be wandering around in the brush.

The leadership and membership of the San Diego Mountain Biking Association (SDMBA) for their commitment to the acquisition and preservation of trails throughout San Diego County.

The leadership and membership of the San Diego County Trails Council (SDCTC) for representing the interests of all of San Diego's non-motorized trail users.

Sunbelt Publications without whom I would have never undertaken something as plainly masochistic as writing an outdoor guidebook.

Bob Martin for knowing every square inch of San Diego County.

Keith Bennett for building trail (legally) where no trail has gone before.

Steve Ferguson for trailside companionship and countless hours of mountain bike techno-therapy.

Jim Hasenhauer of the International Mountain Bicycling Association (IMBA) for his encouragement and guidance.

Greg Lambert for photo assistance.

Gary Hoffman for computer help.

Scott Bringe for demonstrating that it can be done.

And the following federal, state, and local park rangers and trail administrators who make it all happen on the ground:

Anne Carey, Joan Wynn, Ed Heinrich, and Judy Ramsdell of the U.S. Forest Service

Arnold Schoeck of the Bureau of Land Management

Shane Coals of the California Department of Parks and Recreation

Doug Ruth, Robert Wertz, Paul Kucharczyk, David Martinez, and Judy Good of the county of San Diego

Randy Hawley, Tracey Walker, Bill Lawrence, Michael Ruiz, and Dion Heller, of the city of San Diego

Jeff Throop and Tony Smock of the city of Escondido

Sue Pelley of the Olivenhain Municipal Water District

Dennis Bostad of the Sweetwater Authority

Susan Carter, Vickie Touchstone, and Jason Lopez of the San Dieguito River Park

INTRODUCTION

"How greatly does cycling enoble one's spirit, heart and frame of mind! When the cyclist roams freely on his steely steed in the godly world of nature, his heart rises and he bewonders the splendor of creation."

Wilhelm Wolf, 1890

Could it be that mountain biking is a religious experience? Dare we suggest that simply pedaling along a new, an old, or a favorite trail is as lofty a pursuit as the world's great philosophical and theological traditions? You betcha! Just ask a mountain biker.

Everyday, particularly on weekends, mountain bike riders of every age and skill level, and from every walk of life, can be seen making their pilgrimage to the hills and canyons of San Diego County. Whether they're pedaling north on Father Serra Trail, filling their water bottles at Elfin Forest, or speeding east on Highway 8 with a bumper full of bikes, they've all got that certain yearning that only the dirt can satisfy. If they know where to look, they'll find big hills, little hills, mountain streams, sun-drenched cactus or cool pine forest. They'll find rock gardens, box canyons, endless desert vistas, wide-open fire road or—most precious of all—narrow singletrack trail. Some may not actually ride their bikes at all, but will instead spend the day building or repairing trail with other volunteers who share their passion for keeping the backcounty healthy. However they pass the time, they'll most likely end up dirty, smelly, and hungry, but they'll already be planning their next day of worship at the Church of Singletrack Consciousness.

Trail users are drawn to the backcountry for many reasons: some for the exercise, some for the solitude, some for trailside companionship and some simply to commune with the fantastic wilderness that defines so much of the San Diego region. Whatever their motivations, mountain bikers and other trail users all share in some part of the long tradition of rustic adventure that fills the history of our region. From the Kumeyaay Indians to the Spanish explorers to the Mormon Battalion, the backcountry of San Diego has offered an irresistible invitation to men and women to experience our precious wild heritage.

Of course, the dizzying rate of growth of the region's population and economy has been costly to the local environment. Coastal canyons are now coastal communities, pine forests are now "Pine Forest Estates," and old stage routes are now six-lane highways. But San Diegans have not yet completely forgotten the natural environment that brought many of us here in the first place. Southern Californians place great value on outdoor recreation, and although we have presided over much destruction, we have also made efforts to build trail and preserve open space. To the true trail and nature lovers among us, those conservation efforts may seem inadequate. It is easy to look at what once was, and lament the loss of so much of what has made the region special. But we live in a diverse community with many interests and we must focus on the protection of the invaluable public lands that still remain part of our children's inheritance. Mountain bikers and other trail users play a critical role in that effort because our love and respect for trails and open space can lead the way to a place where San Diego's natural splendor exists not only in library picture books but in the real life experiences of adventurers like you.

RESPONSIBLE TRAIL USE

Welcome to the community of responsible trail users. By heading out onto the public trails, you are accepting a certain level of responsibility, not only for yourself, but for the welfare of the trails and public lands as well. I hate to be heavy about this, but as mountain bikers, you and I have got to take this stuff seriously. Mountain biking is a relatively new phenomenon. Trails that were once used exclusively by hikers and equestrians are now the shared legacy of a newly expanded and revitalized group of outdoor enthusiasts.

Like other users, we love the trails and lands that beckon us to adventure. But it is easy to take the public lands for granted and to forget that the narrow strip of dirt under our tires was put in place by pioneering trail builders whose undying commitment and enormous physical and financial efforts created our local trails network. Some trails are built and maintained with public funds, but many, including many of those on public lands, are the fruit of countless hours of volunteerism. Our chronically underfunded public parks and dwindling open space need our support not only as concerned and informed voters, but also as active participants in their management. Mountain bikers have joined the trail using community and we must now help to carry the torch of responsible trail use.

Of course, the public trails belong to you and me just as they belong to the more traditional trail users. But to many, we are an unfamiliar and threatening presence that suddenly appeared in the backcountry. Land managers, trail users, and policy makers have hardly known what to make of us and our exotic machines. Some thought mountain biking was little more than a passing fad, while others thought it meant the end of the world as they knew it.

It is certainly true, although less so today than ten years ago, that mountain bikers have gotten the short end of the stick. Rather than being invited to join and strengthen the trails community, mountain bikers have often been met with some level of suspicion. We were a poorly organized collection of backcountry

The dreaded "NO BIKES" sign. A thing of the past, or the wave of the future? It's up to you.

individualists who were unprepared for the level of concern that our arrival on the trails would provoke among land managers and other trail users. Fears of user conflict, environmental impact and increased liability led to policies that left mountain bikers out in the cold. In the entire California State Park system, every inch of glorious singletrack trail was closed to bikes overnight in 1988. The "No Bikes" signs went up and we were left reeling in disbelief that we had been told to stay away from our very own public trails.

But those were the early days. We mountain bikers can be very proud of our accomplishments over the past decade. Although plenty of shortsighted and discriminatory policies and attitudes are still in effect, access to trails is slowly growing, and user groups have learned the benefits of cooperation over conflict. Reason and science have begun to win out over ignorance and superstition. The path that lies ahead remains treacherous but rideable. California State Park policy still stands, but here in San Diego's Cuyamaca Rancho State Park, for example, singletrack trail is slowly opening to bikes. The leadership of much of San Diego's equestrian and hiking community has invited mountain bikers to join them and we are happy to be their partners. In many ways, San Diego has become a shining example of how trail users and land managers can cooperate with one another toward the common goal of healthy trails and parks. Similar progress has been made in many other areas throughout the country.

How has all this progress come about, you ask? By the efforts of trail users like you. Rather than accept the title of renegades, as we were being branded by those who misunderstood us, mountain bikers decided to take the high road and demonstrate that we are legitimate, responsible, and deserving members of the trail-using community. We have shown that we can not only coexist with other trail users, but our presence strengthens the trails community as a whole. We have brought our enthusiasm, our volunteerism, and our financial resources to the table and, in most cases, we have found friends, not enemies.

These noble efforts have been made through organizations like the International Mountain Bicycling Association (IMBA) and its local affiliate, the San Diego Mountain Biking Association (SDMBA). Mountain bikers also support other user groups through a variety of cooperative programs and events. We have become important partners with public land managers whose trails we have helped to build and maintain. As an individual, you can make all the difference in the world. By riding responsibly and joining your local mountain bike advocacy group, you can help to ensure that the next time you head out to your favorite trail you won't find a "NO BIKES" sign.

S·D·M·B·A

**SAN DIEGO
MOUNTAIN BIKING
ASSOCIATION**

San Diego Mountain Biking Association
P.O. Box 881491
San Diego, CA 92168-1491
Phone: 619/258-9140
http://www2.connectnet.com/~taffe/cycle/SDMBA/SDMBA.html

San Diego County Trails Council, Inc.
P.O. Box 2727
El Cajon, CA 92021-0727
Phone: 619/563-5025
Fax: 619/561-7755

I·M·B·A
INTERNATIONAL MOUNTAIN BICYCLING ASSOCIATION

IMBA
P.O. Box 7578
Boulder, CO 80306-7578
Phone: 303/545-9011
Fax: 303/545-9026
http://www.outdoorlink.com/IMBA/

IMBA'S "RULES OF THE TRAIL"

1. RIDE ON OPEN TRAILS ONLY.

Respect trail and road closures (ask if not sure), avoid possible trespass on private land, obtain permits or other authorization as may be required. Federal and State Wilderness areas are closed to cycling. The way you ride will influence trail management decisions and policies.

2. LEAVE NO TRACE.

Be sensitive to the dirt beneath you. Even on open (legal) trails, you should not ride under conditions where you will leave evidence of your passing, such as on certain soils after a rain. Recognize different types of soils and trail construction; practice low-impact cycling. This also means staying on existing trails and not creating new ones. Don't cut switchbacks. Be sure to pack out at least as much as you pack in.

3. CONTROL YOUR BICYCLE!

Inattention for even a second can cause problems. Obey all bicycle speed regulations and recommendations.

4. ALWAYS YIELD TRAIL.

Make known your approach well in advance. A friendly greeting or bell is considerate and works well; don't startle others. Show your respect when passing by slowing to a walking pace or even stopping. Anticipate other trail users around corners or in blind spots.

5. NEVER SPOOK ANIMALS.

All animals are startled by an unannounced approach, a sudden movement, or a loud noise. This can be dangerous for you, others, and the animals. Give animals extra room and time to adjust to you. When passing horses use special care and follow directions from the horseback riders (ask if uncertain). Running cattle and disturbing wildlife is a serious offense. Leave gates as you found them, or as marked.

6. PLAN AHEAD.

Know your equipment, your ability, and the area in which you are riding – and prepare accordingly. Be self-sufficient at all times, keep your equipment in good repair, and carry necessary supplies for changes in weather or other conditions. A well-executed trip is a satisfaction to you and not a burden or offense to others. Always wear a helmet and appropriate safety gear.

BACKCOUNTRY PREPARATION

Whether you're heading for the deepest recesses of East County or just planning a quick run through Penasquitos Canyon, you need to take your equipment and your safety seriously. Mountain biking can be a dangerous activity and mechanical things are inherently breakable. You're going to fall off the bike once in a while and, occasionally, you're going to break a few bike parts. And as if that weren't enough to worry about, you're also likely to encounter some of nature's prickly and poisonous creatures. Here's some basic information and a few tips.

BIKE STUFF

You've simply got to keep your bike in good working condition. You don't need to be a professional mechanic to learn the basic stuff. Ask a knowledgeable friend or your local retailer to educate you. Don't wait until you arrive at the trailhead to check out the condition of your bike. You should make sure well in advance of ride time that everything is tight and that the parts needing lubrication are nice and slippery. Pay close attention to your chain. Keep it lubed and, if you ride regularly, inspect it and/or replace it approximately once a year. There are few things as unsettling and potentially injurious as breaking a chain in the middle of a power stroke.

You definitely need to carry some tools including at least, but not limited to, the following. All are available at your local bike shop. Don't count on someone else to save you. Know how to use them!

1 spare innertube

1 innertube patch kit

1 air pump

1 set of tire levers

1 set of hex wrenches (allen keys)—Depending on your bike's idiocyncracies, you should carry 4mm, 5mm, and 6mm wrenches.

1 compact "multi-purpose" or "all-in-one" tool - there are many versions on the market. Make sure you know what it does and doesn't contain.

1 chain tool (some multi-purpose tools include a chain tool)

1 spoke wrench that fits YOUR spoke nipples

FLORA AND FAUNA

The plants and animals living in the San Diego region are a fairly benign bunch of creatures. But there are a few things worth knowing about. We've pretty much got just one kind of poisonous snake and it is pretty darn easy to identify (actually, rattlers will generally identify themselves). We've all heard the cliché, "He's more afraid of you than you are of him". Well, I'm here to tell you it ain't so. When a rattler announces himself three feet away from your nice plump calf, you'll immediately know who's more frightened. Several varieties of rattlesnake are quite common throughout the county and should be avoided. You are unlikely to be bitten unless you really blunder into one or are dumb enough to try molesting one for your amusement. Our local rattlers are gorgeous creatures, but they will make your life a misery if they bite and choose to inject you. Common wisdom says baby rattlers are the worst, not only because they are harder to identify but also because, just like human adolescents, they don't have much self-control and tend to inject venom indiscriminately. If you are bitten, stay calm, try to relax, and keep the bite below the level of your heart. If the bite is on a hand or arm, remove any watches, rings, or restrictive clothing. Do not apply a tourniquet and do not apply heat or cold. If you are within two hours of a hospital, you'll probably be just fine. If you are nowhere near civilization and you have access to a snake bite kit, break it out and follow the directions. Do not whip out your pocket knife to attempt the "cut and suck" technique of the past. If you are not alone, send someone for help. Try the cell phone assuming you've got one.

Scorpions are also common in San Diego, but if you're not sticking your fingers or toes under any rocks, you should be fine. The same goes for poisonous spiders.

The mountain lion, also known as cougar, panther, or puma, is tawny-colored with black-tipped ears and tail. Although smaller than the jaguar, it is one of North America's largest cats. Adult males may be more than 8 feet long, from nose to end of tail, and generally weigh between 130 and 150 pounds. Adult females can reach 7 feet in length and weigh between 65 and 90 pounds. Kittens, or cubs, are covered with blackish-brown spots and have darkish rings around their tails. The markings fade as they mature.

Mountain lions are elusive creatures that, despite quite a bit of irresponsible media hype in recent years, very rarely bother humans. We've certainly got quite a few of these magnificent animals in the county, but if you are ever privileged enough to spot one, he or she will likely be beating a hasty retreat. Nevertheless, appropriate behavior in the presence of a mountain lion is pretty much what it would be if you were trying to get your house cat to stop bothering you. Maintain eye contact (they like to attack from the rear), remain upright to make yourself as large and formidable as possible (try holding the bike over your head), be loud and obnoxious but not aggressive, and slowly back off. If worse comes to worst, give 'em all you got. Throwing sticks and rocks is said to be effective. Personally, I've glued a pair of "eyes" to the back of my helmet to avoid being pounced on from the rear. If you are travelling with children, keep them close to you and in sight. In the presence of a lion, pick up the children without crouching or turning away from the animal.

Your most likely contact with a mountain lion will consist of little more than spotting a few paw prints on the trail beneath you. There are a number of animals whose prints you may encounter, and the following figures should help you differentiate among some of the more common creatures with whom we all share the backcountry.

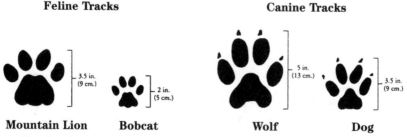

Feline Tracks

3.5 in. (9 cm.)

2 in. (5 cm.)

Mountain Lion   **Bobcat**

Claws seldom show. Generally circular in shape.

Canine Tracks

5 in. (13 cm.)

3.5 in. (9 cm.)

Wolf   **Dog**

Claws usually show. Length generally greater than width.

The most common problem faced by mountain bikers, hikers, and equestrians is also one of the most unpleasant. Poison oak loves San Diego. If you're going to the backcountry, or just a hundred meters down a local coastal canyon, you are almost certain to encounter it. Know it, respect it, never touch it. If you think you're not susceptible, think again. I hadn't reacted to poison oak for 32 years until one day, in 1996, when I became a believer. Although there is recent talk of a pre-exposure treatment, just about the best thing you can do if you think you've come into contact with poison oak is get yourself into a cool shower with lots of soap and water as soon as possible. There is also a good post-exposure cleanser called Tecnu, available at your local pharmacy. Follow the directions. You'll be glad you did.

FIRST AID

Once you start thinking about this one, there's no limit to which paranoia can take you. I've seen folks carrying first-aid kits bigger than a piano. God knows, if you did find yourself in need, you'd be glad you lugged that whole surgical theater out onto the trail with you. But most folks seem to carry very little, if anything at all. The fact of the matter is that most of the injuries you are likely to suffer fall into two groups: 1) those that can probably wait for treatment until you get back home, and 2) those that require your extrication by a professional search and rescue team. Your injuries, let's hope, are very unlikely to fall into the latter category.

Poison oak can have leaves ranging from green to red, or even be leafless. Whatever state it's in, steer clear.

With that said, however, there are a few things you can probably expect to experience on the trail and do something to prepare for. First of all, water is the best piece of safety equipment you can carry. Aside from keeping you hydrated and healthy, the stuff is good for washing off cuts and scrapes. Better still are small, sealed, antibiotic wipes or towlettes available at your local drugstore. Ibuprofen or acetomiophin are also good things that are easy to carry. So too are antihystamine tablets in case you find yourself suffering an allergic reaction to the sting of a bee or other insect. An elastic bandage and a wad of sterile gauze to support sprains and strains, or to cover wounds is a good idea as well. If you wear disposable contact lenses, carry an extra lens to replace the one you accidentally rub out of your eye while wiping your face. Whether or not you wear contact lenses, a small bottle of saline solution can be a life saver if you manage to get something lodged in your peeper. Don't forget your sunscreen. Snake bite kits add a lot of security but are hardly compact. Cell phones are wonderful safety devices, but are little better than a stick of wood if you're outside the service area.

GOOD RIDING

If you do nothing more than ride responsibly and observe IMBA's "Rules of the Trail" as listed above, you can already consider yourself a good mountain biker. But there are a few basic tips that may be helpful on our local trails.

Downhilling—In case you haven't already noticed, the San Diego region has got a lot of steep up and down. Far and away the most important technical tip to remember when descending is don't lock your rear wheel. Aside from being the worst thing you can do to the trail, a wheel that's sliding is a wheel that isn't doing you any good for control. Descending can be a lot less scary if you get used to scooting back on the saddle, even sliding so far back that the saddle is actually under your chest for the steepest descents or drop-offs.

Uphilling—There is nothing more satisfying than finally making it up and over that tricky spot. Unfortunately there is little I can say here that will help you do it. Finding that fine line between a back wheel spin and a front wheelie is all part of the magic of fat tire riding. The only advice that seems to help on steep ascents is to stay on the saddle, bend sharply at the waist and elbows, and pull your chest forward and down toward the handlebar.

Switchbacks—As far as I'm concerned, riding switchbacks, particularly uphill, is mountain biking's highest calling. Switchbacks are sudden, sharp reversals in the direction of the trail alignment, intended to maximize a trail's elevation gain. Although trail builders strive to minimize the number of switchbacks on any trail (they are difficult and costly to maintain), it is sometimes impossible to get from point A to point B without them. When going up, stay on the saddle, stay wide, and aim your front wheel for the outer apex of the turn. When your front wheel has just about run out of trail, cut to the inside of the alignment and pedal hard but smoothly to pull your rear wheel along beneath you. On the way down you'll want to be out of the saddle and slowing down well before the turn. Once again, stay wide as long as possible, then cut your front wheel into the turn and slowly roll into it. Never lock your rear brakes.

Waterbars—Waterbars are those occasionally annoying "obstacles" that you will encounter on many local trails. The vast majority of trail erosion is caused not by trail users but by water running down the trail. Waterbars are intended to divert water from the trail and onto the vegetated hillside which can better withstand or absorb the flow. Most waterbars consist of old railroad ties, but they can also be constructed of rock or, increasingly, flexible material (old conveyor belts) sandwiched between 2×6 lumber. Whether you're going up or down, you should be riding OVER waterbars NOT around them. Attempting to bypass the waterbar widens the trail and compromises the waterbar's effectiveness. Consider each one a challenge. If you're looking for practice, try the Cowles Mountain ride on page 14.

Sand—Although the rides contained in this book keep you away from the soft stuff as much as possible, it's hard to ride in San Diego and not find yourself in sand once in a while. Sand can be very frustrating and calorie intensive. The best advice seems to be pick a relatively low gear, keep your weight back and your legs spinning, maintain forward momentum and minimize any attempts to turn. Heavy riders may find themselves sinking while their skinny riding buddies seem to just float by.

RIDING WITH CHILDREN

Riding with kids can be a blast. There's nothing better than the look on a child's face to remind you of the wonder and adventure that bicycling can bring. Although most of what you need to know about riding with children is just common sense, there are a few things worth reiterating. Keep in mind that children are not always the best backcountry planners. They are relying on you to take care of them in a setting that may be a bit alien, not only to them, but to you as well. It's up to us adults to ensure their safety and enjoyment by taking care of their equipment, setting appropriate limits, and passing on responsible riding practices. The San Diego Mountain Biking Association recommends the following brief tips for riding with kids:

> Don't just wear a helmet, wear a helmet that fits! Every child should have his or her very own, perfectly-adjusted lid. The same goes for all the adults in the group too. A poorly-adjusted helmet can be little more than a distraction and an impairment to a rider's vision. It should take at least 30 minutes to properly adjust the straps on a new helmet. Ask your retailer for help in getting it right. Gloves are another great safety device. Hands are usually the first thing to hit the dirt in the event of a crash.

> Avoid midday heat by riding in the mornings and evenings. Enthusiastic kids can get overheated in a hurry without even realizing it.

> Carry plenty of water or other fluid replacement drinks. Pack a tasty, nutritious snack to share either during a rest stop or after you ride.

Sun protection is essential. When's the last time your eight year old remembered to put on sunscreen before heading out to play? Sunscreen with an SPF of 15 should be standard equipment. A hat securely worn under the helmet is another good way to keep sun off the face.

Always have an emergency plan and be sure every child in the group knows what to do in an emergency. After all, you may be the one who needs help. Carry a first aid kit containing at least those items listed in the Backcountry Preparation section above. Make a plan in case you get separated.

Ride at your child's pace. Let them lead the ride but stay close behind to offer direction, coaching, encouragement, and praise. Take plenty of rest stops to enjoy your "quality time."

Bring a camera to record some great memories.

USING THIS BOOK

If ever there were such a thing as a labor of love, putting together a trail guide is it. My hope is that the following pages serve not simply to prevent you from getting lost, but will take you to places of inspiration. The rides listed here cover nearly every corner of the county and expose you to trails ranging from easy to masochistic. Needless to say, every possible ride in the San Diego region has not been included, not only because the task of collecting such information would be too great, but because mountain biking is, by its very nature, a process of exploration and discovery. I have recommended some routes that only hint at the adventure that may await you around the next corner. Although each recommended ride is a completely self-contained, start-to-finish route, you may find yourself mid-ride staring longingly at an enticing trail that leads off in a direction not mentioned in the ride description. Sometimes those trails go forever, sometimes they go nowhere. Welcome to mountain biking. Have a good time.

Of course, there are a few trails you should definitely not be exploring. Throughout the book, I have tried to indicate those trails or areas that should be avoided. Crossing onto private land is just plain wrong unless you have the owner's blessing or you are traveling on a public trail easement. When in doubt, don't do it. Aside from risking the individual legal consequences, angering private land owners can do a lot of damage to our legitimate efforts to acquire more trails and access in the future.

Perhaps the biggest mistake a mountain biker can make is riding on trail that may be public but is closed to mountain bikes. As you read above, access to trails is a critical issue for mountain bikers. Nothing sets back our progress toward greater acceptance than illegal or reckless trail riding. Land managers, other trail users, and policy makers see riding on closed trails as the most direct evidence of bicyclists' irresponsibility. Of course, all trail user groups, including hikers and equestrians, contain a small number of idiots who don't mind screwing everything up for the rest of us. As the new kids on the block, we mountain bikers need to be on our best behavior. However ridiculous and unfair a particular trail closure may be (and there are plenty of examples), civil disobedience on the trails is a recipe for disaster. Instead, contact the San Diego Mountain Biking Association and become part of the solution.

One particular trail that you should make special note of is the Pacific Crest Trail (PCT), a 2,638 mile odyssey running north/south from Canada to Mexico. Several of the rides listed in this book intersect sections of the PCT as it winds its way across San Diego County. The PCT is open to hiking and equestrian use only. Bicycles are prohibited.

As often as possible, I have recommended routes that allow you to complete a full loop. Needless to say, any loop can be abbreviated by simply turning around and heading back the way you came. Of course, you will need to make the appropriate adjustment to the mileages I've listed for each ride. You will no doubt notice that I am a big advocate of climbing. For those loops or partial loops where your direction of travel can be varied, I have generally recommended the direction that has you climbing on as much dirt as possible. I like it like that. Nothing increases my appreciation of a trail and its environment more than riding up it. The whole phenomenon of the car "drop-off" or "shuttle ride" gives cross-country riders like me the heebie-jeebies.

Speaking of riding on dirt, I could not avoid including many rides that involve some amount of paved road. Pure dirt rides exist but are a bit of a rarity. I hope you'll find that it's worth putting up with some pavement in order to get to the good stuff.

After making a few introductory statements about each ride, I have provided a detailed ride description in tabular form. I have found that organizing rides in this way provides the easiest and most efficient way for riders to quickly glance at the text and stay on track. After all, you didn't buy a mountain bike to improve your reading skills. A number of terms appear along with each ride description and they are explained or defined below:

ROUTE TYPE—This simply gives you the big picture of the ride's layout. Although there are a few slight variations, "out-n-backs" take you back and forth along the same route while "loops" take you in a full circle back to your starting point. I've listed several "lollipops" (Table Mountain, Elfin Forest, Suycott Wash, Grapevine Canyon), which are basically loops stuck onto the far end of an out-n-back. You know what I mean.

DISTANCE—All distances are for the entire ride described and are listed in miles. Let's face it, we're never going to adopt the metric system. If your bike is not equipped with a computer, you'll need to do your best to estimate your mileage and attempt to fit your estimates to both the ride description and the maps. Each ride shows cumulative distance, incremental distance and distance to finish. Cumulative distance is simply the total mileage you will have traveled at each point in the ride description. Incremental distances are intended to save you the trouble of constantly doing the math in your head to figure out how far you'll be going before you need to start worrying about your next big turn. Because not every item in the ride description is a critical juncture, incremental distances are only listed when they really matter. Generally, I've shown incremental distances whenever you actually need to make a turn. Distance to finish is also intended to spare your math skills by letting you know how much further you'll be riding before finishing the recommended route.

RIDING TIME—This one is a bit tricky because everybody likes to move at a different pace. Generally, the total riding times listed are what it took me to finish the ride with plenty of time-outs for snack foods, nature viewing, and an occasional bike repair.

ELEVATION GAIN—These are estimates based on evaluation of detailed topographical maps, but they probably have a pretty good margin of error. As you know, or are about to discover, 500 feet of climbing on loose skree ain't the same as 500 feet of climbing on nicely packed dirt, so take these elevation gain/loss figures with a grain of salt.

AEROBIC SCALE—As the name indicates, this factor is intended to describe the level of sustained cardiovascular strain that you'll be facing. On a scale of 1 to 5, "1" is just pedaling along while "5" is marathon training.

BURN FACTOR—Although the Aerobic Scale tells most of the story, it doesn't do a very good job of capturing the occasional desperate burn that accompanies most mountain bike riding. The Burn Factor is a way of describing how much anaerobic lunging you'll do. On a scale of 1 to 5, "1" means no big surprises while "5" means you'll find yourself repeating phrases like "We're going up THAT?" A high Burn Factor can mean quite a bit of portage.

SCARE-O-METER—Finally, I've attempted to give you some idea of how frightened you can expect to be. On a scale of 1 to 5, "1" means relax, while "5" means you may need several years of therapy for a complete emotional recovery.

MAPS

I have provided a map for nearly every ride described in the text. Those rides not accompanied by a map should be so plainly obvious that getting lost would be a miracle. My intention has been to keep the text and the maps uncluttered by details that aren't strictly relevant to the recommended ride. Although some of the less-than-critical topograhical or landmark features have been excluded, none of the maps have been shortened, squished, or otherwise abbreviated in terms of their relative dimensions. Each map shows the recommended route (indicated by solid black arrows) as well as much of the other trail within the map area. Each map also indicates the rough inclination of the trail along the recommended route. The arithmetic inclination symbols (+, ++, +-, -, =) must be viewed relative to the direction of travel and, needless to say, must be reversed if your direction of travel changes.

Although the book you now hold in your hand is all you really need to complete every ride listed, I nevertheless encourage you to build your own library of

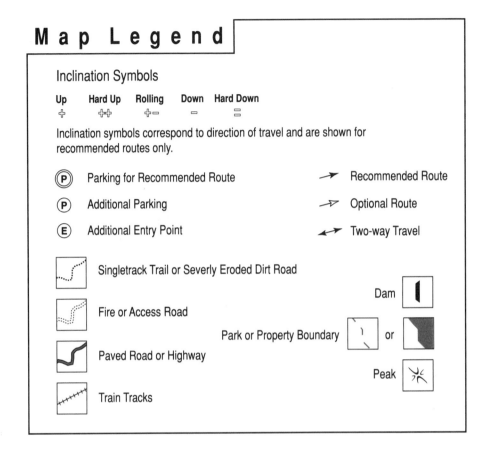

local maps and guide books from other sources. You probably own one or more trail maps or guides already and it's always a good idea to educate yourself as much as possible before heading out. I have included a brief recommended reading list in the appendix.

RIDE RECOMMENDATIONS BY SKILL LEVEL

Making recommendations according to skill level can be a bit tricky. Some novices want nothing that isn't completely flat, while other novices are happy in the rough stuff even if they end up having to carry the bike most of the day. Some experts won't touch a trail that burns fewer than a trillion calories, while others are thrilled just to be on the dirt. The following guidelines are intended to keep all riders, whatever their skill or fitness level, out of trouble, on the bike, and hungry for more.

If you are brand-spanking new to mountain biking, there are a few things you ought to do before heading for the dirt. Assuming you've done everything necessary to make sure your bike is in good working condition, you first should familiarize yourself with your bikes shifting, breaking and overall feel by taking a few leisurely rides on your local bike path or parking lot. By the time you take your first ride on the dirt, you should be so well acquainted with your bike's workings that shifting and breaking are almost second nature. You should be equally expert at changing a flat tire and using the other tools in your toolkit. Now you're ready to get filthy.

BEST NOVICE RIDES

The coastal canyons (particularly rides 1a, 1b, and 2) are good places to get started. Although not exactly flat, you won't find too much to worry you. The "Grasslands" area in the northeast part of Mission Trails Park (see the map on page 17) is also a safe place to explore and expand the limits of both your bicycle and body. Ride 5 (Lake Hodges) is also suitable, but introduces a bit more climbing. After you've got a couple of rides under your belt, I highly recommend an excursion to the Big Laguna Trail (ride 12a) where you can safely test your newly developed aerobic and bike-handling skills on one of the forest's most beautiful and forgiving singletrack trails. If you'd like a taste of the county's drier, eastern parts, McCain Valley (ride 18) will do the trick without killing you. Although the ride, as described in the text, is quite long, you can easily truncate it by simply turning around at any point and heading back to the car. Don't forget that the McCain Valley Road is open to motorized vehicles and should be ridden with caution, particularly if you've got children along on the ride.

BEST INTERMEDIATE RIDES

If you're ready to expand your horizons beyond the novice rides recommended above, grab a buddy and head for Cuyamaca Rancho State Park (ride 13a and 13b). Both of these rides will take your lungs and bike-handling skills to the next level without leaving you in a lurch. Closer to the coast, Sycamore Canyon in the north (ride 6) and Sweetwater Reservoir in the south (ride 10) should also make you happy. For a bit of desert exposure, the Table Mountain area (ride 19a) is a dramatic change of scenery. When you're ready to push a bit further, both Daley Ranch (ride number 8) and Elfin Forest (ride 9) can take you there.

BEST EXPERT RIDES

Making recommendations for expert riders is a silly business. As an expert, I still love to ride on nearly everything that I enjoyed as a novice. If you think certain rides are beneath your skill and strength level, I urge you to revisit some of your old haunts and rediscover the things that got you hooked in the first place. But if you need a challenge, San Diego County has got it. Ride 13c, although not the most technical of routes, is calling your name. The 36 miles of Palomar Mountain (ride 15b) should also give you a kick in the pants. In the Lagunas, the Kitchen Creek/Thing Valley loop (ride 12d) is sure to make you breathe, as is the old standard, Noble Canyon (ride 12b). And you haven't seen it all if you haven't seen the highest point in San Diego County - Hot Springs Mountain in the Los Coyotes Indian Reservation (ride 17).

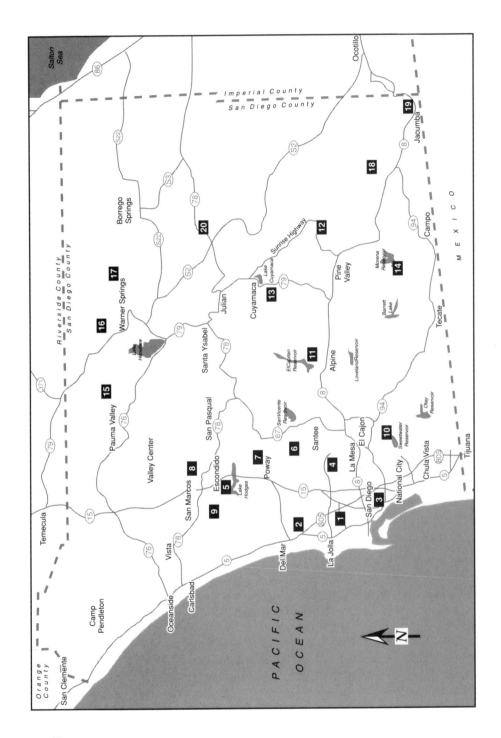

THE RIDES

COASTAL CANYONS AND FOOTHILLS

1 The Tri-Canyons 1
1a Marian Bear Memorial Park (San Clemente Canyon) 2
1b Rose Canyon Open Space Park 4
1c Tecolote Canyon Natural Park 7

2 Los Penasquitos Canyon Preserve 8

3 Balboa Park–Florida Canyon 11

4 Mission Trails Regional Park 13
4a Cowles Mountain 14
4b Suycott Wash Loop 18
4c North Fortuna Peak 20

5 Lake Hodges–San Dieguito River Park 22

6 Sycamore Canyon Open Space Preserve/ Goodan Ranch 26

7 Lake Poway and Twin Peaks 29

8 Daley Ranch–Escondido 34

9 Elfin Forest 37

10 Sweetwater Reservoir 41

MOUNTAINS

11 Anderson Truck Trail 47

12 Laguna Mountains 50
12a Big Laguna Trail 50
12b Noble Canyon/Indian Creek Trail 53
12c Sheephead Mountain Road 57
12d Kitchen Creek/Thing Valley Loop 59

13 Cuyamaca Rancho State Park 61
13a Grand Loop 63
13b Oakzanita Peak 66
13c Boulder Creek Loop Deluxe 68

14 Lake Morena/Corral Canyon 72

15 Palomar Mountain 75
15a West Side–Nate Harrison Grade 77
15b East Side 78

16 Indian Flats 80

17 Los Coyotes Indian Reservation 83

TRANSITIONAL AND TRUE DESERT

18 McCain Valley 89

19 Jacumba Mountains 90
19a Table Mountain 92
19b Valley of the Moon 95

20 Anza Borrego Desert 96
20a Three Canyons— Rodriguez/Oriflamme/Chariot 98
20b Grapevine Canyon 99

COASTAL CANYONS
AND FOOTHILLS

1 THE TRI-CANYONS

Despite their immediate proximity to some of San Diego's most congested urban neighborhoods, the Tri-Canyon Parks do a good job of convincing you that you've got at least one foot in the outback. Although most of the riding is not extremely challenging, all three canyons do convey the rugged nature of San Diego's disappearing coastal canyon topography. Each park has multiple access points, and their locations near the coast make them rideable year round. All three parks, with their creek-level trail systems, often suffer during heavy winter rains, so it's always a good idea to check with a ranger before heading out in the wet season. As is typical of most urban rides, the Tri-Canyon Parks are visited heavily by trail users of every persuasion, some of whom may not always tread as lightly as they should. Be gentle, follow the rules, and don't forget to volunteer with the park or a local user group to help keep the trails healthy. Aside from seasonal or temporary closures, the parks are generally open from sunrise to sunset.

1a MARIAN BEAR MEMORIAL PARK (SAN CLEMENTE CANYON)

ROUTE TYPE	Out-n-Back
DISTANCE	4.4 miles
RIDING TIME	1 hour
ELEVATION GAIN	200 ft
AEROBIC SCALE	1/5
BURN FACTOR	1/5
SCARE-O-METER	1/5
LAND MANAGER	City of San Diego - Department of Parks and Recreation
INFORMATION	619-581-9952 or 619-581-9961

Though mostly within earshot of Highway 52, the thick oak, sycamore, and willow which typify San Clemente Canyon provide just enough of a screen to make this convenient urban ride a worthwhile escape. Consisting of 467 acres running east-west between I-5 and I-805, the Park's existence is a testament to the resolve of community activists, led by Marian Bear, who refused to let the construction of Highway 52 obliterate the beautiful canyon that had served man and nature so well for thousands of years. The canyon is quite flat, but the often rocky tread can put your bike handling skills to the test as you occasionally scramble along the creek bed. Although the canyon is criss-crossed by a spider's web of single-track trails, bicyclists are generally encouraged to remain on the main access trails running the length of the canyon. The attached map shows a small number of finger trails which rise up out of the drainage and are also open to bikes, at least on a provisional basis. It's always a good idea to check with a ranger regarding current trail status.

THE DRIVE

From either the east or west, take Highway 52 and exit at Clairemont Mesa Blvd./Regents Road. The parking area is just south of Highway 52, at the bottom of the canyon, and can be entered coming from either direction. The ride described below starts from the extreme east end of the parking area and covers the eastern reach of the park. To the west, the park continues approximately 0.75 miles before fizzling out at the train tracks parallel to I-5. At that point, you can access the Rose Canyon Open Space Park by going North through the concrete wash just east of the train tracks. In addition to the main parking area off of Clairemont Mesa Blvd./Regents Road, Marian Bear Park is also accessible from Genesee Avenue, where a smaller parking facility is located at the bottom of the canyon just east of Genesee.

RIDE 1a

MARIAN BEAR MEMORIAL PARK

INCREMENTAL DISTANCE	CUMULATIVE DISTANCE	DESCRIPTION OF RIDE	DISTANCE TO FINISH
	0.0	Start measuring from the extreme east end of the Regents Road parking area on the east side of Regents Road. Head EAST toward I-805.	4.4
	0.6	Pass the Biltmore Trail on your right and, shortly, the Standley Trail on your left. These trails are currently open and are worth a bit of careful exploration.	3.8
	1.0	Pass under Genesee Avenue and pass the Genesee Avenue parking area to your left. Continue up the canyon on the main trail.	3.4
2.2	2.2	The trail begins to meander badly as it approaches I-805. Turn around and head back the way you came. Any further east may have you staring down the barrel of an M-16 while you donate your bike to the U.S. Marine Corps at MCAS Miramar.	2.2
2.2	4.4	Back at the car near Regents Road.	0.0

Marian Bear Memorial Park,
Rose Canyon Open Space Park—Rides 1a, 1b

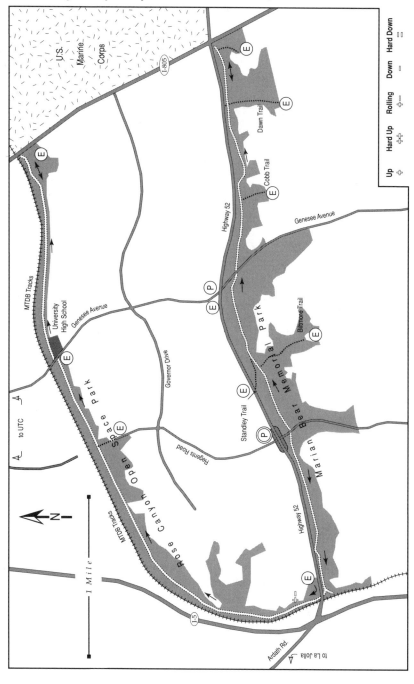

San Clemente Canyon looking east.

1b ROSE CANYON OPEN SPACE PARK

ROUTE TYPE	Out-n-Back
DISTANCE	9.8 miles
RIDING TIME	1 hour
ELEVATION GAIN	250 ft
AEROBIC SCALE	1/5
BURN FACTOR	1/5
SCARE-O-METER	1/5
LAND MANAGER	City of San Diego Park and Recreation Department
INFORMATION	619-581-9952

Like Marian Bear Park, Rose Canyon stretches east-west between I-5 and I-805 as it skirts along the condominium developments of the UTC area just to the north. The park parallels the MTDB train tracks as they follow Rose Canyon inland. A bit drier than San Clemente Canyon, Rose Canyon offers grassier, more-exposed vistas, but an otherwise similar riding experience in terms of level of effort. Steer clear of the railway. Every year, several people discover that the front end of an MTDB commuter train has only one setting: "puree."

THE DRIVE

Although the park can be accessed from several points (see map), the ride described below begins at the main parking area for Marian Bear Park at the intersection of Highway 52 and Clairemont Mesa Blvd./Regents Road (see the Marian Bear description above). San Clemente Canyon drains into Rose Canyon at the west end and this is the recommended access point for all of Rose Canyon as it stretches northeast. Park at the Marian Bear parking area and begin riding from the extreme west end of the parking lot.

RIDE 1b

ROSE CANYON OPEN SPACE PARK

Incremental Distance	Cumulative Distance	Description of Ride	Distance to Finish
	0.0	Start measuring from the extreme west end of the Marian Bear Park parking area at the intersection of Highway 52 and Regent Road. Head WEST toward I-5.	9.8
	0.8	As the trail approaches I-5, cross the creek and continue NORTH through the concrete wash. You have just joined Rose Canyon. Continue up the main trail which follows the train tracks.	9.0
	3.5	Turn LEFT on Genesee and immediately cross the street toward University City High School. The trail continues adjacent to the school on the north side.	6.3
4.9	4.9	When you hit the I-805 overpass, turn around and return whence you came. East of the 805 wait the U.S. Marines with the authority to confiscate bikes.	4.9
4.9	9.8	Back at the car.	0.0

Tecolote Canyon Natural Park—Ride 1c

1c TECOLOTE CANYON NATURAL PARK

ROUTE TYPE	Out-n-Back
DISTANCE	12.2 miles
RIDING TIME	1.5 hour
ELEVATION GAIN	450 ft
AEROBIC SCALE	2/5
BURN FACTOR	3/5
SCARE-O-METER	2/5
LAND MANAGER	City of San Diego Park and Recreation Department
INFORMATION	619-581-9952

Like her two sisters to the north, Tecolote Canyon offers a glimpse into coastal San Diego's rugged past. Winding its way up from Mission Bay to Clairemont Mesa Blvd., the canyon runs primarily north/south, with a number of small finger canyons rising to the mesas on either side. Tecolote definitely features quite a bit of up and down as you roll across the short, but occasionally very steep, pitches that define the walls of the canyon. Like the other coastal canyons, Tecolote has several entry points (see map), but is best accessed from the eastern end of Tecolote Road, not far from Mission Bay. Stop in at the Nature Center near the trailhead to gain an appreciation for what an important role these disappearing canyons have long played in San Diego's coastal life.

THE DRIVE

Take I-5 and exit at Sea World Drive/Tecolote Road. Take Tecolote Road east approximately 1 mile until it ends at the Tecolote Canyon Natural Park Nature Center. Park here.

RIDE 1c

TECOLOTE CANYON NATURAL PARK

INCREMENTAL DISTANCE	CUMULATIVE DISTANCE	DESCRIPTION OF RIDE	DISTANCE TO FINISH
	0.0	Start measuring from the Tecolote Canyon Nature Center at the eastern terminus of Tecolote Road. Head NORTHEAST on the main access road up the canyon.	12.2
	1.1	Pass the pipeline facility on your left. The trail will now take you over a set of short but steep rollers as you parallel the Tecolote Canyon Golf Course. Generally bear LEFT, remaining close to the golf course.	11.1

continues

TECOLOTE CANYON NATURAL PARK *(continued)*

INCREMENTAL DISTANCE	CUMULATIVE DISTANCE	DESCRIPTION OF RIDE	DISTANCE TO FINISH
2.1	2.1	With the golf course still to your Left, take the trail dropping down LEFT across the creek. You should emerge next to the pro-shop between the golf course and the driving range. Take the pavement of Snead Avenue NORTH away from the golf course toward Mt. Acadia Avenue.	10.1
	3.1	RIGHT on Mt. Acadia and immediately LEFT back onto the trail to continue up the canyon.	9.1
	4.1	As you approach Balboa Ave. bear LEFT and climb parallel to the road.	8.1
	4.5	Emerge onto Balboa Ave. and continue LEFT (north) up Balboa toward the Clairemont Drive intersection. Cross Balboa at Clairemont Drive and head SOUTH on the Balboa sidewalk, looking for the continuation of the trail on your LEFT at mile 5.0.	7.7
3.6	5.7	Bear LEFT at the "T" and soon take the short, hard climb to the North Clairemont Recreation Center at mile 6.1. Now turn around and head back where you came from.	6.5
6.1	12.2	Back at the car.	0.0

2 LOS PENASQUITOS CANYON PRESERVE

ROUTE TYPE	Out-n-Back
DISTANCE	11.6 miles
RIDING TIME	1 hour
ELEVATION GAIN	300 ft
AEROBIC SCALE	2/5
BURN FACTOR	2/5
SCARE-O-METER	1/5
LAND MANAGER	City of San Diego Park and Recreation Department
	County of San Diego Park and Recreation Department
INFORMATION	619-538-2480

Los Penasquitos Canyon is one of San Diego's busiest urban parks and offers some worthwhile and scenic riding opportunities. The canyon's proximity to the crowded Golden Triangle area, along with the fact that it is accessible from both ends, has ensured a high level of public use. Visitors are well advised to avoid the

Los Penasquitos Canyon Preserve—Ride 2

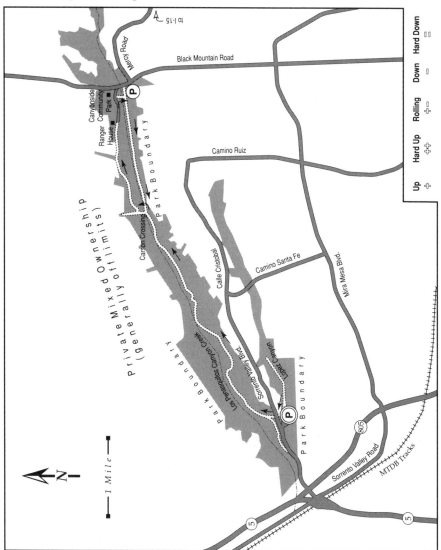

park on weekends if at all possible. The park suffers greatly during heavy rains and often remains closed to the public for quite some time following serious weather. Calling ahead is always a good idea. Generally, the preserve is open from 8:00 AM to sunset.

Unfortunately, current park policy restricts cyclists to the main access roads connecting the two ends of the park. None of the several miles of singletrack trail are open to mountain bikes. Yes, that even means that you cannot legally enter or leave the park via any of the many side spurs that connect to the mesa on the north side, most of which is in private ownership anyway. If you feel that the policy barring cyclists from the singletrack that IS within the park boundaries is unfair, you can get involved by contacting park management or the San Diego Mountain Biking Association. Just about the worst thing you can do for the cause of increased access is ride illegally on closed trail or during periods when the entire park is closed.

The canyon can be entered from either Sorrento Valley Blvd. (Lopez Canyon staging area) or from Black Mountain Road where it intersects Mercy Road. Parking is available at both ends, but there is a $1 per vehicle fee at the Black Mountain Road entrance administered by the county. The ride described below begins at the west end of the canyon from the Sorrento Valley Blvd. parking area but can be ridden in either direction.

THE DRIVE

From I-805 traveling north

Exit at Sorrento Valley Road and follow the signs to the right and under the highway. At 1.4 miles, turn RIGHT at Sorrento Valley Blvd. Continue an additional 1.0 miles and turn RIGHT into the parking area for Los Penasquitos Canyon Preserve (Lopez Canyon staging area). The trail begins at the east end of the staging area.

From I-5 traveling north

Exit at Sorrento Valley Road. Turn LEFT at the T and immediately RIGHT at Sorrento Valley Blvd. Cross the train tracks and continue 1.0 miles. Turn RIGHT into the parking area for Los Penasquitos Canyon Preserve (Lopez Canyon staging area). The trail begins at the east end of the staging area.

RIDE 2

LOS PENASQUITOS CANYON PRESERVE

INCREMENTAL DISTANCE	CUMULATIVE DISTANCE	DESCRIPTION OF RIDE	DISTANCE TO FINISH
	0.0	Start from the east end of the parking area and follow the main trail LEFT under Sorrento Valley Blvd.	11.6
	0.5	Bear RIGHT and continue east parallel to Los Penasquitos Creek.	11.1
3.5	3.5	Bear LEFT and cross to the north side of the creek at Carson Crossing.	8.1
0.2	3.7	Turn RIGHT onto the main service road parallel to the creek and continue up the canyon.	7.9

| 2.1 | 5.8 | Arrive at the Canyonside Community Park parking area off of Black Mountain Road. You can now return the way you came or look for the access road crossing back to the main access road on the south side of the creek, which you can take all the way back to the Sorrento Valley parking area. | 5.8 |
| 5.8 | 11.6 | Back at the car in Lopez Canyon. | 0.0 |

3 BALBOA PARK–FLORIDA CANYON

ROUTE TYPE	Mixed
DISTANCE	~3 miles
RIDING TIME	~1 hour
ELEVATION GAIN	~200 ft
AEROBIC SCALE	2/5
BURN FACTOR	2/5
SCARE-O-METER	2/5
LAND MANAGER	City of San Diego Park and Recreation Department
INFORMATION	619-235-1121

Balboa Park is hardly a secret, but mountain biking opportunities are. Few people are aware that the park offers some rugged, albeit compact, singletrack fun. Significant improvements were made to the Florida Canyon hiking and biking trail network in early 1997, and the result is a perfectly respectable system of narrow and sometimes challenging trails less than a minute from downtown San Diego. If you've never experienced this aspect of Balboa Park, now's the time to go pay your respects to the city's noble efforts to preserve what is perhaps the only remaining natural topography and ecology within earshot of the convention center.

THE DRIVE

Although the park can be accessed from several points (see map), you may want to park your vehicle at the tennis courts at the northeast end of the canyon, off of Morley Field Drive and Jacaranda Place.

THE RIDE

I offer no recommended ride in Florida Canyon other than to suggest that you start from the Dog Park entrance and generally make your way around the trail system in a clockwise direction. You should feel free to explore the network of often narrow trails on both sides of Florida Street. Just keep an eye out for cars as you cross the road. Drivers aren't expecting to see a mountain bike pop out of the bushes so close to downtown.

Balboa Park–Florida Canyon—Ride 3

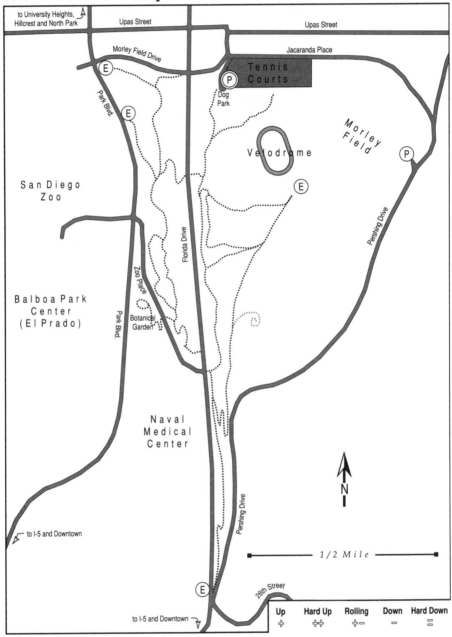

4 MISSION TRAILS REGIONAL PARK

Mission Trails Regional Park, including Cowles Mountain and Lake Murray, is one of the largest urban parks in the country. Situated between the communities of Tierrasanta, Santee, and La Mesa, the park has many entry points and a wide variety of riding opportunities. For most San Diegans, the park can easily be reached by car in less than thirty minutes, making it one of the most popular riding and hiking destinations in the county. Bordered by State Route 52 to the north and I-8 to the south, the park presently consists of nearly 6,000 acres of grassland, chaparral, riparian forest, and rugged canyons and peaks. The park's five highest points are the peaks of North Fortuna (1291'), South Fortuna (1094'), Kwaay Pay (1194'), Pyles Peak (1379') and Cowles Mountain (1591', the highest point in the city of San Diego).

The park also contains the Old Mission Dam Historic Area, a nationally registered historic landmark dating to 1810, when Kumeyaay Indian labor, under the direction of Spanish missionaries from Mission San Diego de Alcala, began construction of an adobe-lined flume to transport water from the San Diego River downstream 5.5 miles to the mission. Remnants of the original dam project are clearly visible. Visitor facilities at the Old Mission Dam area underwent significant improvements in early 1997, making it an excellent starting point for rides and hikes throughout the park.

The park's main visitor facility is located near the intersection of Mission Gorge Road and Father Junipero Serra Trail, which parallels the San Diego River through the park. Vehicle traffic on Father Serra Trail is limited to daylight hours, and travel is allowed in only one direction from the visitor center, north (upstream) toward the Mission Dam area. Non-motorized traffic can travel in either direction. The Visitor and Interpretive Center is open daily from 9:00 AM to 5:00 pm and is well worth visiting for an introduction to the park's history and ecology. The center can be reached by phone at 619-668-3275.

The three rides described below are intended to provide you with an introduction to the park and its varied terrain. Most of the park's trails are currently open to bicycle use, and you should feel free to explore the many corners of the park on your own. Although the park has several entry points (see map), all of the rides described below start at the Visitor and Interpretive Center at the south end of Father Serra Trail. If you would like to begin your ride elsewhere, simply subtract the appropriate mileage from the distances indicated below. Novice riders may want to restrict themselves to the "grasslands" area of the park, which is accessed most easily from the northeast side of the park near the Old Mission Dam area.

THE DRIVE

From the north

Take 52 east, exit at Mission Gorge Road and turn RIGHT. In another 0.75 miles, Father Serra Trail will fork off to your right. You can follow it to the Mission Dam parking area or remain on Mission Gorge Road, which will take you over the hill and down to the Visitor Center on your right in approximately 2.5 miles.

From Downtown San Diego area

Take I-8 east. Exit at Mission Gorge Road and turn LEFT (north). Continue 1.0 miles and turn RIGHT (northeast) at the T intersection. You will still be on Mission Gorge Road. Continue an additional 3.0 miles until you pass Jackson Drive. Take the next LEFT on Father Junipero Serra Trail and LEFT again into the Visitor Center parking area, or simply park on Father Serra Trail below the Visitor Center. There is no fee to park, but the gate to the visitor center parking area generally locks at sunset, so don't get stuck.

4a COWLES MOUNTAIN

ROUTE TYPE	Modified Loop
DISTANCE	10.9 miles
RIDING TIME	1.5 hours
ELEVATION GAIN	900 ft
AEROBIC SCALE	4/5
BURN FACTOR	4.5/5
SCARE-O-METER	2.5/5
LAND MANAGER	City of San Diego Park and Recreation Department
INFORMATION	619-668-3275

The lower half of this ride takes you through the coolest area of the park, where much of the trail remains in partial shade due to the area's tall chaparral and northern exposure. The most remarkable aspect of this ride is the inordinately large number of waterbars you'll encounter during the early part of the ascent. Although initially a bit tedious, you'll soon discover the challenge of trying to find a rhythm that will allow you to clear each step. It's the perfect place to explore the Zen of curb-hopping.

The recommended route includes quite a bit of pavement that provides a warm-up before the climbing starts and creates a full loop with enough miles in it to give you a workout. The uphill dirt component is challenging (waterbars) and fairly narrow initially, then widens into a smooth but occasionally very steep access road for the final assault. The Barker Way singletrack that I recommend on the way down can be a serious technical slap-in-the-face if you're having anything less than a great day.

COWLES MOUNTAIN

Incremental Distance	Cumulative Distance	Description of Ride	Distanc to Finish
	0.0	Start from the Visitor Center by continuing EAST on the pavement of Father Serra Trail passing through the center of the park.	10.9
2.2	2.2	Turn LEFT onto Mission Gorge Road.	8.7
0.6	2.8	Turn RIGHT on Rancho Fanita Drive.	8.1
0.6	3.4	Continue STRAIGHT across the T intersection, past the wooden barrier and onto the singletrack. Cross the small creek bed in front of you and immediately bear LEFT across the meadow. Public tennis courts will be to your left.	7.5
0.2	3.6	Turn RIGHT onto the pavement of Mesa Drive. The road will soon turn to dirt as you enter the park.	7.3
0.6	4.2	Turn RIGHT onto the singletrack which im-- mediately drops down to cross the creek. Bear LEFT on the opposite side of the creek to begin your ascent.	6.7
0.8	5.0	LEFT at the trail intersection to continue climbing. (A right turn takes you back down into Santee and should be kept in mind as a potential return route.)	5.9
0.5	5.5	Turn RIGHT onto the main dirt access road.	5.4
	5.7	Make a mental note as you pass the Barker Way singletrack on your left.	5.2
0.9	6.4	Welcome to the top of Cowles Mountain. When you're done catching your breath and checking out the view, start back down the way you came.	4.5
0.7	7.1	Turn RIGHT onto Barker Way singletrack. If you prefer to avoid this difficult and technical trail, simply pass the Barker Way turnoff and continue to descend all the way on the main access road. Both lead to the same place.	3.8
	7.4	Bear LEFT downhill. As you approach the bottom of the hill there are a variety of	3.5

continues

COWLES MOUNTAIN *(continued)*

INCREMENTAL DISTANCE	CUMULATIVE DISTANCE	DESCRIPTION OF RIDE	DISTANCE TO FINISH
		small trails that will lead you to the edge of the park.	
0.9	8.0	You are now back on the pavement of Barker Way street. Make your way one block further southeast (away from the park) and turn RIGHT on Cowles Mountain Blvd.	2.9
1.2	9.2	RIGHT on Golfcrest Drive.	1.7
1.1	10.3	LEFT on Mission Gorge Road.	0.5
0.6	10.9	RIGHT on Father Junipero Serra Trail and back to the Visitor Center.	0.0

Steve Ferguson on the north side of Cowles Mountain—188 waterbars and still smiling.

Mission Trails Regional Park—Cowles Mountain, Suycott Wash Loop, North Fortuna Peak—Rides 4a, 4b, 4c

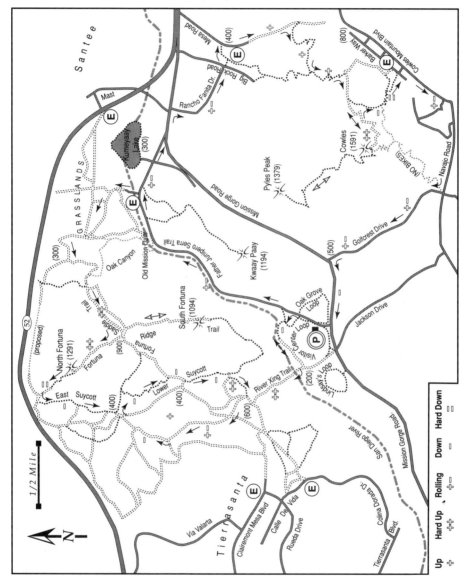

4b SUYCOTT WASH LOOP

ROUTE TYPE	Lollipop
DISTANCE	6.0 miles
RIDING TIME	1.5 hours
ELEVATION GAIN	800
AEROBIC SCALE	4/5
BURN FACTOR	3/5
SCARE-O-METER	2.5/5
LAND MANAGER	City of San Diego Park and Recreation Department
INFORMATION	619-668-3275

This ride also starts at the Visitor Center but quickly puts you on the dirt as you cross (ford) the San Diego River and begin climbing the access road toward Tierrasanta. The main water crossing can be impassable during or soon after heavy rain, and you may be forced to enter from the Mission Dam area (via the Fortuna Mountain saddle) or from the intersection of Colina Dorada and Calle De Vida in Tierrasanta.

You'll spend much of the early part of the ride on fairly wide access roads, but after climbing up into the park and following the ridgeline to Four Corners, you'll descend to the fun and semi-technical Suycott Wash singletrack. Suycott Wash will finish with a technical scramble out of the canyon and then the big downhill back to the San Diego River and the Visitor Center.

John Rice, Lorene Rice, and the author doing the conga line in the shadow of Fortuna Mountain.

RIDE 4b

SUYCOTT WASH LOOP

Incremental Distance	Cumulative Distance	Description of Ride	Distance to Finish
	0.0	Head NORTH (away from Mission Gorge Road) on the Visitor Center Loop Trail which starts from the gate at the bottom of the driveway leading up to the Visitor Center. Follow the main trail DOWN and LEFT to the main river crossing.	6.0
	0.2	Bear LEFT away from Father Serra Trail.	5.8
0.9	0.9	Bear RIGHT and cross the San Diego River if possible. Begin climbing.	5.1
0.5	1.4	Bear RIGHT. A left turn would take you out of the park toward Tierrasanta.	4.5
	1.5	Continue climbing but make note of the Suycott Wash/Fortuna Mountain singletrack on your right. You'll be emerging from that trail in about 30 minutes.	4.5
	1.8	Continue NORTH toward the concrete cylinders on top of the hill. Continue NORTH staying on top of the bluff but as far RIGHT (east) as possible. The road will eventually descend to Four Corners at 2.7.	4.1
1.3	2.7	Welcome to Four Corners. Continue STRAIGHT through the intersection on the West Fortuna trail but immediately look for the Suycott Wash singletrack trail on your RIGHT. Take it south down into the canyon.	3.2
0.5	3.2	RIGHT on East Suycott Wash singletrack.	2.8
0.4	3.6	RIGHT on South Suycott Wash fire road.	2.4
0.1	3.7	Bear LEFT onto South Suycott Wash singletrack.	2.2
0.4	4.1	Bear RIGHT immediately after the picnic area. Trail sign points to Calle De Vida.	1.8
0.1	4.2	Bear LEFT and climb the short steep singletrack.	1.7
0.3	4.5	Turn LEFT and return to the Visitor Center the way you came in.	1.5
1.5	6.0	Welcome back to the Visitor Center.	0.0

4c NORTH FORTUNA PEAK

ROUTE TYPE	Loop
DISTANCE	9.2
RIDING TIME	2 hours
ELEVATION GAIN	1700
AEROBIC SCALE	4/5
BURN FACTOR	5/5
SCARE-O-METER	3/5
LAND MANAGER	City of San Diego Park and Recreation Department
INFORMATION	619-668-3275

This ride has a large burn factor but rewards you handsomely with the view from North Fortuna Peak and the very fun singletrack descent to the north end of Suycott Wash. Standing between you and the vista, however, is so called "Blood Hill," which can be either a source of inspiration or frustration, depending upon your mood. Either way, it's well worth giving it a go. Once again, you'll begin from the Visitor Center at the other end of the park, but you'll be glad you had the warm-up.

RIDE 4c

NORTH FORTUNA PEAK

INCREMENTAL DISTANCE	CUMULATIVE DISTANCE	DESCRIPTION OF RIDE	DISTANCE TO FINISH
	0.0	Start from the Visitor Center by continuing EAST on the pavement of Father Serra Trail passing through the center of the park.	9.2
1.8	1.8	Just past the Old Mission Dam parking area, turn LEFT onto the short paved descent to the low water crossing. Continue NORTH across the "grasslands" parallel to Oak Canyon on your left.	7.4
0.8	2.6	Bear LEFT on the main access road toward Fortuna Mountain.	6.6
0.3	2.9	Follow the access road as it curves LEFT away from Highway 52.	6.3
0.2	3.1	Bear LEFT at the "Y" toward Fortuna Mountain.	6.1
	3.2	Crest the hill and descend toward Oak Canyon/ Fortuna Mountain/Suycott Wash.	6.0
	3.5	Pass the Oak Canyon Trail on your left (closed to bikes but a beautiful walk).	5.7

	3.6	Cross (ford) the creek and pass the continuation of Oak Canyon Trail on your right (open to bikes and worth a try). Start climbing toward the Fortuna Mountain Saddle on so called "Blood Hill."	5.6
	3.6	Pass the even steeper power line road to your left.	5.6
1.0	4.1	Welcome to the "top." Try to breathe. Turn RIGHT and continue climbing on the ridge toward Fortuna Peak. Left turn option takes you to South Fortuna Mountain, which is well worth a visit and can actually connect you to the south end of Suycott Wash.	5.1
	4.7	Access road ends. Continue STRAIGHT onto the singletrack descending toward Highway 52.	4.5
	5.1	Join the access road and continue to descend LEFT toward Suycott Wash.	4.1
1.2	5.3	Turn LEFT on the singletrack slightly up and to your left (easy to miss).	3.9
	5.6	Continue STRAIGHT toward Rim Trail/Suycott Wash.	3.6
0.7	6.0	Just before reaching Four Corners, turn LEFT onto the Suycott Wash singletrack.	3.2
0.4	6.4	Turn RIGHT on East Suycott.	2.8
0.4	6.8	Turn RIGHT on access road toward South Suycott/Calle de Vida.	2.4
0.1	6.9	Bear LEFT on singletrack toward South Suycott Wash Trail/San Diego River.	2.3
0.5	7.4	Turn RIGHT at the picnic area toward Calle de Vida/San Diego River.	1.8
0.0	7.4	Turn LEFT and climb the singletrack out of the canyon.	1.8
0.3	7.7	Turn LEFT on access road and LEFT again to descend to San Diego River. Check your brakes!	1.5
	8.3	CROSS (ford) the San Diego River and bear LEFT to climb back up to the Visitor Center.	0.9
1.5	9.2	Back at the car.	0.0

Bob Martin doing it in Oak Canyon, Mission Trails Park

5 LAKE HODGES–SAN DIEGUITO RIVER PARK

ROUTE TYPE	Out-n-Back
DISTANCE	14.2 miles
RIDING TIME	2 Hours
ELEVATION GAIN	800 ft
AEROBIC SCALE	2/5
BURN FACTOR	2/5
SCARE-O-METER	1/5
LAND MANAGER	San Dieguito River Park Joint Powers Authority
INFORMATION	619-235-5440

The San Dieguito River begins at Volcan Mountain north of Julian and eventually drains into the Pacific Ocean through the San Dieguito Marsh near Del Mar. In an effort to preserve the river valley's natural resources, and to provide recreational opportunities for San Diego County's outdoor-loving residents, several of the local governments along the river corridor joined with the County of San Diego in the hope of establishing the river valley as a protected open space. With the support of trail users like you, the vision of a "Coast to Crest" trail covering the nearly 55 miles from Del Mar to Volcan Mountain may someday become a reality.

Although opponents of the park have managed to slow the process, certain elements of the park plan have come together nicely. The Lake Hodges trail system is a popular North County escape for hikers, bikers, equestrians, bird watchers, and trail runners, not to mention the boaters, anglers, and wind surfers who utilize the lake itself. For mountain bikers, the Lake Hodges area offers several miles of trail and dirt road ranging from easy to moderately difficult. The bulk of the trail system generally follows the shoreline between I-15 and Del Dios Highway, and takes you on a mostly level path through the rolling chaparral and grassland that cover the steep hills bordering the lake. There are a number of attractive singletrack trails that parallel the main path as it follows the shoreline. But despite the fact that they are used quite frequently by the public, those narrow trails and their short connectors are almost entirely on private land outside

Looking west along the main trail on the north shore of Lake Hodges.

Lake Hodges–San Dieguito River Park—Ride 5

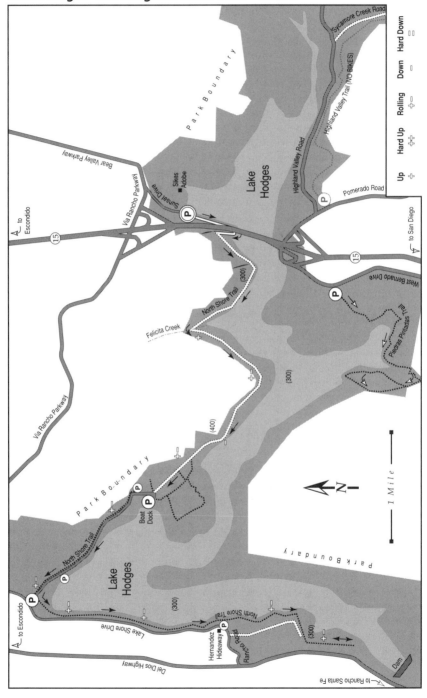

the park boundary. They should be avoided. The trail system sees heavy weekend use and, as usual, is best visited Monday through Friday.

Although the ride described below puts you on the north shore of the lake, where the majority of the trails are located, the Piedras Pintadas Trail on the south side is also well worth exploring. Unfortunately, you will need to drive to the south side by taking I-15 to West Bernardo Drive. Plans are under way for a north/south passage, but the freeway is currently the only connection.

THE DRIVE

Take I-15 north and exit at Via Rancho Parkway. Turn RIGHT (EAST) off the ramp and RIGHT again on Sunset Drive. Continue approximately 0.25 mile and park where Sunset Drive ends at the trailhead. Your ride begins here.

RIDE 5

LAKE HODGES–SAN DIEGUITO RIVER PARK

INCREMENTAL DISTANCE	CUMULATIVE DISTANCE	DESCRIPTION OF RIDE	DISTANCE TO FINISH
	0.0	Start measuring from the Sunset Drive parking area. Head SOUTH on the paved or dirt path toward the Lake. The trail will pass under I-15 and head north briefly.	14.2
0.6	0.6	Turn LEFT onto the main trail, which still has paved remnants.	13.6
	1.6	Cross (ford) Felicita Creek and climb the rocky section back toward the Lake.	12.6
	2.6	Stay on the wide, main trail as it heads left down toward the lake. The slightly more technical singletrack to the right is unofficial and technically off-limits.	11.6
	3.4	Arrive at the boat dock parking area. Cross the parking lot and turn RIGHT along the lake shore on either the paved road or the dirt frontage on either side.	10.8
4.1	4.7	Arrive at the Lake Drive parking area. Bear LEFT on the singletrack leaving the parking lot toward the lake shore. The singletrack now continues along the west shore of the lake. The trail becomes a bit schizophrenic for the next 2 miles. Just keep yourself between Lake Shore Drive and the water.	9.5

continues

LAKE HODGES–SAN DIEGUITO RIVER PARK *(continued)*

INCREMENTAL DISTANCE	CUMULATIVE DISTANCE	DESCRIPTION OF RIDE	DISTANCE TO FINISH
	5.9	Arrive at the parking area across the street from Hernandez Hideaway. Beer. The trail leaves from the parking area, once again following the lake shore.	8.3
2.4	7.1	The trail begins to fizzle as you approach the Lake Hodges Dam area. Turn around and return whence you came.	7.1
7.1	14.2	Back at the car.	0.0

6 SYCAMORE CANYON OPEN SPACE PRESERVE/GOODAN RANCH

ROUTE TYPE	Lollipop
DISTANCE	6.3 miles
RIDING TIME	2 hours
ELEVATION GAIN	900 ft
AEROBIC SCALE	3/5
BURN FACTOR	3/5
SCARE-O-METER	2/5
LAND MANAGER	County of San Diego Department of Parks and Recreation
	California Department of Fish and Game
	City of Poway
	City of Santee
INFORMATION	619-694-3030 (County) or 619-679-5469 (Blue Sky Ecological Reserve)

Whether you're a novice or an experienced rider, Sycamore Canyon offers a satisfying blend of hard work and handsome reward. Occupying one of the few yet-undeveloped canyons west of Highway 67, the relatively new Sycamore Canyon Open Space Preserve, including the adjoining Goodan Ranch property, is like a big brother to the flatter, less technical coastal canyons described previously. You'll find rolling hills, thick chaparral, oak, and, you guessed it, sycamore grove. The preserve is managed by the county while the adjoining Goodan Ranch property is jointly administered by State Fish and Game, San Diego County, and the cities of Poway and Santee.

Mountain bike use is currently welcomed on several miles of the preserve's dirt access roads. Unfortunately, current county policy excludes bicycles from nearly all of the canyon's singletrack trails - including the beautiful Martha's Grove trail. Anything that is not a wide, graded access road should generally be considered off-limits to bicycles unless otherwise posted open. Always check

Sycamore Canyon Open Space Preserve/Goodan Ranch—Ride 6

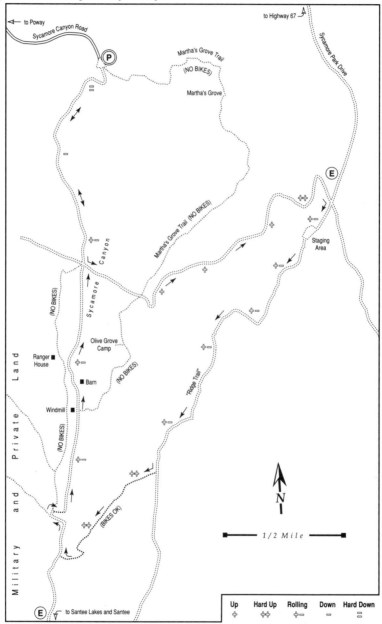

to Poway
to Highway 67
Sycamore Canyon Road
Sycamore Park Drive
P
Martha's Grove Trail
(NO BIKES)
Martha's Grove
E
Martha's Grove Trail (NO BIKES)
Staging Area
Sycamore Canyon
(NO BIKES)
Olive Grove Camp
Ranger House
(NO BIKES)
Barn
"Ridge Trail"
Military and Private Land
Windmill
(NO BIKES)
N
1/2 Mile
(BIKES OK)
E
to Santee Lakes and Santee

Up	Hard Up	Rolling	Down	Hard Down

with a ranger or the county's Parks Department for the latest news. There are currently two exceptions to the "singletrack closed" rule and the recommended ride described below will take you on both of them.

The joint preserve is best accessed from the north via Sycamore Canyon Road in Poway, but it can also be entered from Santee in the south via Pebble Beach Drive just west of the Santee Lakes recreation area. You may also enter from the east via Sycamore Park Drive off of Highway 67 approximately two miles south of the Highway 67 intersection with Poway Road (S4). Although the park is open for public use seven days a week, the Sycamore Park Drive gate is locked on weekdays to prevent motorized access.

Depending on your skill level, you may want to abbreviate the relatively challenging route described below. The recommended ride starts at the Sycamore Canyon Road parking area and immediately has you descending into the canyon on the main access road. You'll then be climbing to the Sycamore Park Road staging area on the eastern side of the park before descending once again to the main access road on the floor of the canyon.

THE DRIVE

Via I-15

Exit at Poway Road and travel EAST through the center of Poway. At 4.7 miles bear RIGHT on Garden Road as Poway Road curves to the left. Continue on Garden Road an additional 1.0 miles and turn RIGHT on Sycamore Canyon Road. Continue an additional 2.2 miles (the road is presently dirt but has been slated for paving in the near future). Park at the Goodan Ranch/ Sycamore Canyon Open Space Preserve parking area.

The park can also be entered from Santee via Pebble Beach Drive by riding pretty much due north on the most well-established dirt access roads that don't cross onto military or private land on either side. This area is very poorly signed, so take care not to get lost. Access to the park off Highway 67 is via Sycamore Park Drive approximately two miles south of the Highway 67 intersection with Poway Road (S4). The entrance road is easy to miss. The gate is not open to motorized traffic on weekdays so you may want to drive around to the Sycamore Canyon Road entrance in Poway.

		RIDE 6	

SYCAMORE CANYON OPEN SPACE
PRESERVE/GOODAN RANCH

INCREMENTAL DISTANCE	CUMULATIVE DISTANCE	DESCRIPTION OF RIDE	DISTANCE TO FINISH
	0.0	Start measuring from the parking area. Take the main access road down into the canyon.	6.3
0.9	0.9	Turn LEFT (southeast) onto the access road.	5.4

	1.1	Pass the Martha's Grove trail on your left. Continue straight ahead and begin climbing toward the ridge.	5.2
1.3	2.2	Turn RIGHT on the access road (Sycamore Park Road). Left would take you to Highway 67.	4.1
	2.3	Pass straight through the staging area and continue on the rocky fire road following the ridge south.	4.0
1.5	3.7	The fire road fades. Turn RIGHT onto the steep, singletrack (yes, it is open to bikes) and descend to the floor of the canyon.	2.6
0.6	4.3	Cross the gate and turn RIGHT onto the access road.	2.0
0.1	4.4	Turn LEFT, cross the creek, and immediately turn RIGHT. Pass through the gate and immediately turn RIGHT again onto the singletrack (yes, it's open) toward the windmill.	1.9
	4.9	Pass the windmill on your left and cross the wooden bridge. Continue straight on the main access road toward the barn.	1.4
	5.4	Continue straight at the intersection and head back to the parking area the same way you came in.	0.9
1.9	6.3	Back at the car.	0.0

7 LAKE POWAY AND TWIN PEAKS

ROUTE TYPE	Mixed Loop
DISTANCE	11.4 miles
RIDING TIME	3 Hours
ELEVATION GAIN	1500 ft
AEROBIC SCALE	2.5/5
BURN FACTOR	3/5
SCARE-O-METER	2/5
LAND MANAGER	City of Poway
INFORMATION	619-679-5423 or 619-679-5417

The city of Poway is one of the small but growing number of local communities across the country who have begun to take trails seriously. Hiking, biking, and horse riding are as American as apple pie, but creating or simply preserving open space and trail alignments have always been tremendous challenges for small communities as they wrestle with issues of population growth and economic development.

Fortunately, the citizens of Poway have seen fit to prevent their quality of life from sliding into the urban abyss by acknowledging that trails, and the recreational opportunities they provide, are worth supporting. Halleluya!

The result of Poway's enlightenment is a community trails system for all to enjoy. Although much of the trail network is extremely urban (i.e., in very close proximity to fully developed areas of the city), you can nevertheless hike, pedal, or trot in nearly unbroken rhythm for hours on end. You may find yourself passing within five feet of someone's backyard BBQ party and, ten minutes later, be feeling anything but urban as you dodge rattlesnakes and heatstroke on the treacherous slopes of Mt. Woodson. The beauty of an urban trails system is in its accessibility and in the public support for trails that such accessibility can generate.

Today, Poway boasts 60 miles of trail, with more to come. The ride recommended below is intended to give you a taste of what Poway has to offer, by showing you some of the more urban (Del Poniente Trail) as well as the more rustic and challenging (Lake Poway and Mt. Woodson) aspects of the trails network. As the map shows, you can easily shorten the recommended ride by eliminating one part or the other. You will be spending the vast majority of the ride on the dirt, some of which can be quite steep and loose. Remember, a lot of folks (and animals) use the Poway trails, so don't expect to be alone. Always yield trail.

The ride starts at the Lake Poway parking area where, unless you are a Poway resident, you will need to pay a $4.00 parking fee. Obviously, you can avoid the

Terry Callan circumambulating at Lake Poway.

fee by biking in, but there's nothing wrong with spending a few bucks to support a city that supports trails.

THE DRIVE

Take I-15 North and exit at Ted Williams Parkway. Turn RIGHT (East) and continue 2.4 miles to Twin Peaks Road. Turn RIGHT and continue an additional 2.2 miles to the signal at Espola Road. Turn LEFT and climb 2.1 miles to Lake Poway Road. Turn RIGHT and continue to the kiosk at the top of the hill. Pay the fee and park.

RIDE 7

LAKE POWAY AND TWIN PEAKS

Incremental Distance	Cumulative Distance	Description of Ride	Distance to Finish
	0.0	Start from the Lake Poway parking area. The trail begins from the southeast corner of the parking lot. Immediately bear RIGHT onto the singletrack of the upper trail heading counterclockwise around the lake.	11.4
	0.4	Trail drops down to join the main trail, still following the lakeshore.	11.0
	0.8	Pass the Mount Woodson Trail on your right. If you'd like to try the very challenging option of climbing Mount Woodson, it will add 3 miles, 1000 feet, and about 2 grunts to your overall ride.	10.6
1.2	1.2	Bear RIGHT to remain on the Lake Poway Trail. Left deadends at the dam. You'll now descend sharply beneath the dam.	10.2
0.7	1.9	Turn LEFT toward the dam and begin climbing. A Right turn at 1.9 would send you toward the Blue Sky Ecological Reserve, which is open to all but mountain bikers. If that doesn't seem fair, get in touch with your local trails access group and let the City of Poway and SD county know how you feel.	9.5
	2.3	You've just about recovered all of your elevation. Continue STRAIGHT past the trail on your right.	9.1
	2.5	Continue STRAIGHT on the main trail, ignoring the lefts that, if you've had enough, will take you back to the parking area via the lake shore. Your trail will now leave the lake behind you as it descends parallel to Lake Poway Road.	8.9

continues

LAKE POWAY AND TWIN PEAKS *(continued)*

INCREMENTAL DISTANCE	CUMULATIVE DISTANCE	DESCRIPTION OF RIDE	DISTANCE TO FINISH
1.3	3.2	Cross Espola Road and continue on the right shoulder of Lake Poway Road. Climb steadily.	8.2
0.7	3.9	Turn LEFT off of Lake Poway Road and back onto the Del Poniente Trail, following the fence line.	7.5
0.6	4.5	Turn RIGHT to remain on Del Poniente Trail	6.9
	4.6	Cross Midland Road.	6.8
	4.8	Jog RIGHT, following the trail through the fence.	6.6
	5.2	STRAIGHT past the access road on your left. It leads to the eastern of the Twin Peaks.	6.2
	5.3	STRAIGHT past the access road on your left. It leads to the western of the Twin Peaks. You will now be descending toward Pomerado Road.	6.1
1.2	5.7	Bear RIGHT at the "Y" and continue to traverse north between Pomerado Road on your left and the hills to your right.	5.7
0.7	6.4	The trail drops you onto the pavement behind the Gateway Retirement Home. Turn RIGHT and follow the pavement to the continuation of the trail on your right. Follow the split rail fence down to Pomerado Road.	5.0
0.3	6.7	Turn RIGHT onto the pavement of the Pomerado Road bike path.	4.7
0.7	7.4	Turn RIGHT on Avenida La Valencia and immediately LEFT onto the trail.	4.0
0.3	7.7	Turn RIGHT following the drainage upstream, then bearing LEFT at the fence.	3.7
0.5	8.2	Turn RIGHT onto the pavement of Espola Road.	3.2
1.1	9.3	Espola Road widens to 2 lanes. Immediately look RIGHT and take the continuation of the trail.	2.1
	9.8	Cross Summer Sage Road.	1.6
0.7	10.0	Turn RIGHT onto the pavement of Espola Road	1.4
0.5	10.5	Turn LEFT on Lake Poway Road.	0.9
0.9	11.4	Back at the car.	0.0

Lake Poway and Twin Peaks—Ride 7

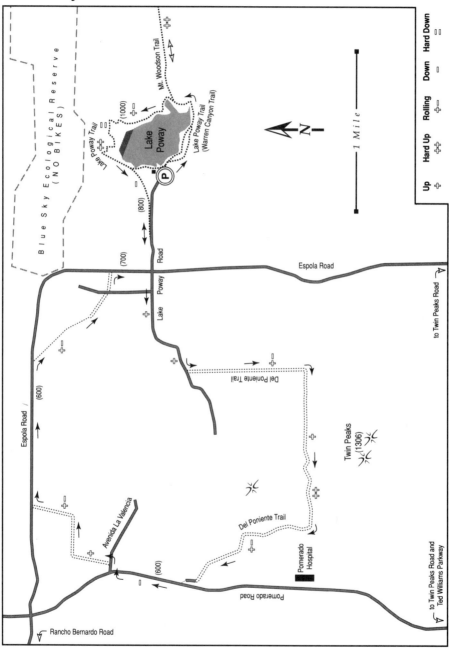

8 DALEY RANCH–ESCONDIDO

ROUTE TYPE	Mixed Loop
DISTANCE	9.0
RIDING TIME	2.0 hours
ELEVATION GAIN	1800
AEROBIC SCALE	3.5/5
BURN FACTOR	3/5
SCARE-O-METER	2.5/5
LAND MANAGER	City of Escondido Public Works Department
INFORMATION	760-741-4680 (Dixon Lake Recreation Area)

In the spring of 1997, the City of Escondido added a crowning jewel to its local trails network with the opening of approximately 3000 acres recently acquired from the Daley family. Saved from becoming just another tile-roofed housing tract, the park offers oak grove, pristine chaparral, meandering meadow, riparian vistas, and great hiking and riding. Adjacent to Dixon Lake just north of Escondido, the Daley Ranch is easily accessible and offers a variety of highly recommended mountain biking opportunities. Novices will find the park quite challenging but not impossible. More experienced riders will be grinning uncontrollably. The newness of the park makes it a potential flashpoint for user conflict, so it is critical that we bicyclists impress the local rangers with how well we can share this wonderful park with other trail users.

The recommended ride puts you mostly on fairly narrow access roads with some bumpy and steep sections mixed in. There are many options within the park and, in accordance with your skill and energy level, you should feel free to embelish on the route described below. You're sure to notice that there is quite a bit (about 12 miles) of attractive singletrack within the park, much of which is currently open to bikes. The accompanying map does not show most of the singletrack trail, but you're sure to have a good time searching it out on your own. Check with park rangers before riding on anything that you suspect may be closed.

THE DRIVE

Take I-15 NORTH from San Diego and exit at El Norte Parkway. Turn RIGHT (East) and continue 2.7 miles to La Honda Drive. Turn LEFT and continue an additional 0.9 miles up the hill to the end and park on the left, across from the entrance to Dixon Lake. Your ride starts here.

Daley Ranch–Escondido—Ride 8

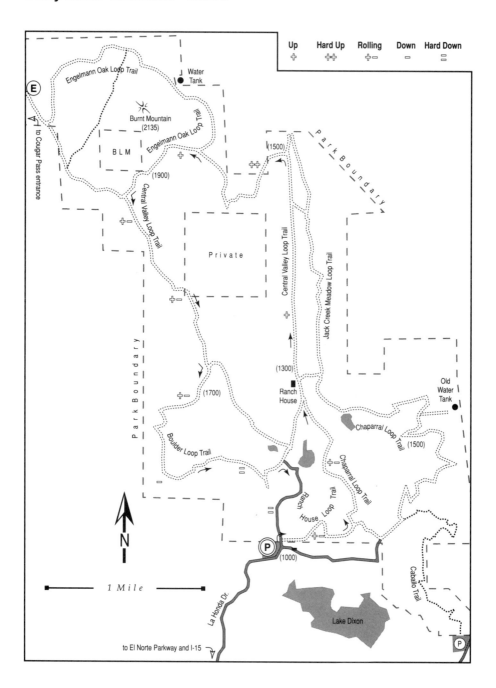

RIDE 8

DALEY RANCH–ESCONDIDO

Incremental Distance	Cumulative Distance	Description of Ride	Distance to Finish
	0.0	Start from the parking area and head uphill through the Daley Ranch gate. Immediately turn RIGHT onto Ranch House Loop Trail.	9.0
0.7	0.7	Turn LEFT and up the short grunt to remain on Ranch House Loop Trail. A Right turn option takes you up the eastern ridge on Chaparral Loop Trail and will also drop you at the ranch house in approximately 2.5 miles.	8.3
0.9	1.6	Turn RIGHT onto the main road and pass the ranch house on your left.	7.4
	1.8	After passing the ranch house, continue STRAIGHT up the valley on Central Valley Loop Trail.	7.2
1.6	3.2	Bear LEFT (continuing straight would take you to the park boundary) to remain on Central Valley Loop Trail. Enjoy the big grunt ahead.	5.8
1.1	4.3	Turn LEFT on Engelmann Oak Loop Trail. (right on Engelmann Oak Loop would take you 3.5 miles around Burnt Mountain)	4.7
	4.9	Pass the Engelmann Oak Loop Trail turnoff on your right.	4.1
1.9	6.2	Turn RIGHT on Boulder Loop Trail.	2.8
	6.8	Bear LEFT, away from private property boundary.	2.2
1.6	7.8	Bear LEFT toward Dixon Lake.	1.2
0.1	7.9	Turn RIGHT on the main road to return to the parking area. If you prefer to continue riding, you can simply turn left instead of right and head back up past the ranch house, bearing right to follow the Chaparral Loop Trail through the southwest corner of the park. This option will add approximately 3 miles of nice riding to your day.	1.1
1.1	9.0	Back at the car.	0.0

9 ELFIN FOREST

ROUTE TYPE	Lollipop
DISTANCE	10.8 miles
RIDING TIME	2-3 hours
ELEVATION GAIN	2000 ft
AEROBIC SCALE	4/5
BURN FACTOR	4/5
SCARE-O-METER	3/5
LAND MANAGER	Olivenhain Municipal Water District
INFORMATION	760-753-6466

The Elfin Forest Recreation Reserve (previously known as Mount Israel) is a relatively new addition to the constellation of local pedaling opportunities and is well worth visiting if you're looking for a challenging but accessible year-round ride. Located in the steep coastal mountains between Encinitas and Escondido, Elfin Forest is one of the county's few truly mountainous rides that doesn't require a long drive east. Although warm in summer, the park's proximity to the coast often provides just enough breeze to take the edge off the heat. The riding is rugged and varied as you rise from the riparian zone along Escondido Creek to the dry chaparral of the hilltops. Critters abound in the thick brush and, if you're lucky, you may even spot a mountain lion.

Managed by the Olivenhain Municipal Water District, the park welcomes mountain bikes on much of its approximately 12 miles of fire road and singletrack trail. Crowding can be a problem in this relatively compact and increasingly popular park, so it's important for us mountain bikers to be on our best behavior. As usual, weekday rides are highly recommended.

Most of the riding is on singletrack trail ranging from easy and firm to steep and loose. The initial ascent from the parking area is the only way into the park for all users and can get a bit crowded. It's quite steep and serves as an effective filter for trail users who may not be up to the challenge of the park's occasionally steep pitches. It is well worth struggling to the top, however, where things flatten out a bit and the vistas open up in all directions. Water is available at the parking area and at the picnic facilities on top. Trail maps are posted intermittently, and shade structures are even available at the major lookouts.

The ride described below, although still the recommended route, is somewhat tentative. The Water Authority plans to flood a good portion of Oak Valley sometime over the next three years. The result will inundate several trails and may turn the Lakeview Ridge Trail into an out-n-back rather than the loop described below. The land managers need to hear from mountain bikers and other trail users that we'd like to see more trail—not less—and that we are here to help toward that goal.

Valley View Ledge Trail looking west at Elfin Forest.

THE DRIVE

Via I-15 North

Exit at 9th Avenue/Auto Parkway and head WEST at the bottom of the ramp. Continue an additional 0.2 miles and turn LEFT on 9th Avenue. Continue an additional 0.7 miles and follow the road LEFT onto Hale. Continue 0.2 miles and turn RIGHT onto Harmony Grove Road. After another 0.2 miles turn LEFT to remain on Harmony Grove. Continue 0.5 miles and bear LEFT again to remain on Harmony Grove Road. Continue 2.5 miles and look for the Elfin Forest parking area on your left below the road. Check the signs to avoid having your vehicle locked in the parking area after hours. Additional parking is available off Harmony Grove Road just east of the park entrance.

Elfin Forest—Ride 9

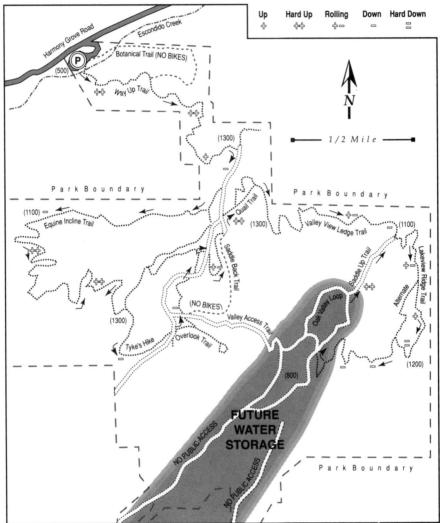

Via I-5 North

Exit at La Costa Avenue and head EAST 3.6 miles. Turn LEFT on Rancho Santa Fe Road. Continue 1.5 miles and turn RIGHT on Questhaven Road. Continue 1.7 miles and turn RIGHT on Elfin Forest Road. Continue 2.3 miles and turn LEFT onto Harmony Grove Road. Continue an additional 1.6 miles and look for the Elfin Forest parking area on your right below the road. Check the signs to avoid having your vehicle locked in the parking area after hours. Additional parking is available off Harmony Grove Road just east of the park entrance.

ELFIN FOREST

Incremental Distance	Cumulative Distance	Description of Ride	Distance to Finish
	0.0	Start climbing on the Way Up Trail.	10.8
	0.4	Pass the Self-Guided Botanical Trail on your left. Not open to bikes but well worth a stroll later on if you've got the energy.	10.4
1.3	1.3	Turn RIGHT onto North Point Loop fire road.	9.5
0.1	1.4	Turn RIGHT on Equine Incline singletrack.	9.4
0.1	1.5	Bear RIGHT at the fork to remain on Equine Incline.	9.3
1.9	3.4	Turn RIGHT, remaining on Equine Incline.	7.4
0.2	3.6	Bear RIGHT toward the Elfin Forest Overlook. Depart the overlook via Tyke's Hike Trail.	7.2
	3.9	Pass through the gate and across the fire road to continue descending on Tyke's Hike.	6.9
0.5	4.1	Turn LEFT to continue on Tyke's Hike.	6.7
	4.2	Cross fire road and continue on Tyke's Hike.	6.6
	4.4	Cross fire road and continue on Tyke's Hike.	6.4
	4.5	Pass the Equine Incline connector trail on your left.	6.3
	4.5	Cross fire road and continue on Tyke's Hike	6.3
0.7	4.8	Turn LEFT on the fire road. Right turn would take you immediately to the Ridge Top Picnic Area with bathrooms and water.	6.0
	4.8	Turn RIGHT on the fire road. Ignore the second Equine Incline connector directly in front of you.	6.0
0.2	5.0	If you're pooped, you can turn left and return to the parking area via the Way Up Trail. For more fun, however, continue STRAIGHT at the intersection onto the Quail Trail rising to the northeast. Immediately bear LEFT onto the Quail Trail Alternate to circumvent the straight pitch directly ahead of you.	5.8

	5.2	Join the Valley View Ledge Trail and continue along the ridge to the Escondido Overlook.	5.6
	6.3	Continue STRAIGHT across the drainage and begin climbing on the Lakeview Ridge Trail.	4.5
	6.7	Pass the Lakeview Ridge Trail Alternate on your right.	4.1
2.0	7.0	Arrive at the Lake Hodges Overlook and begin your descent into Oak Valley.	3.8
0.7	7.7	Turn RIGHT on the Oak Valley Loop Trail heading back up the canyon toward the Saddle Up Trail.	3.1
	8.0	Join the Saddle Up Trail and continue climbing.	2.8
0.5	8.2	LEFT on Valley View Ledge Trail back the way you came.	2.6
1.1	9.3	Turn RIGHT at the bottom of the Quail Trail to return to the parking area via the Way Up Trail.	1.5
1.5	10.8	Back at the car.	0.0

10 SWEETWATER RESERVOIR

ROUTE TYPE	Out-n-Back
DISTANCE	7.2
RIDING TIME	2 hours
ELEVATION GAIN	900 ft
AEROBIC SCALE	3/5
BURN FACTOR	4/5
SCARE-O-METER	2/5
LAND MANAGER	Sweetwater Authority U.S. Department of the Interior - Fish and Wildlife Service County of San Diego Department of Parks and Recreation
INFORMATION	619-420-1413 (Sweetwater Authority) 760-930-0168 (U.S. Fish and Wildlife Service) 619-472-7572 (S.D. County - Sweetwater Summit Site)

If you've been looking for trails in the south county, Sweetwater's got 'em. Lucky for us, the good people at the Sweetwater Authority, which manages the reservoir, have seen fit to provide us trail users with several miles of fun singletrack trail and access road. Otherwise surrounded by private holdings, the Sweetwater Authority manages a narrow buffer zone of land around the reservoir to protect the water and biological resources of the lake from contamination. There is

Sweetwater Reservoir—Ride 10

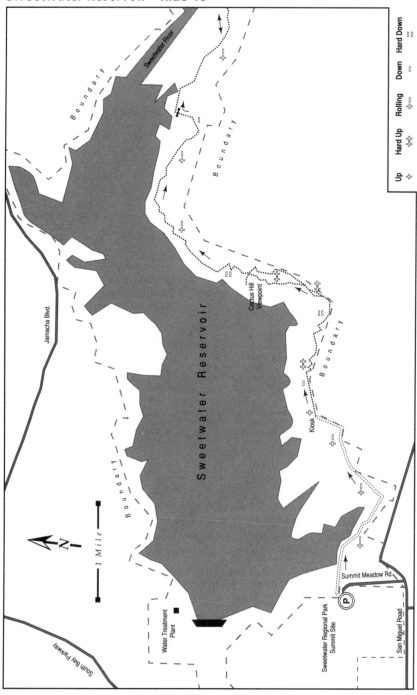

no public access to the water itself. For the entire ride, you'll be following the somewhat obtrusive fence as it parallels the lakeshore.

The ride described below is a nearly 7.4 mile out-n-back along the southern boundary of the reservoir. Although the ride starts at the Sweetwater Park Summit Site managed by San Diego County, you'll quickly cross onto Sweetwater Authority land for the rest of the ride. The recommended route definitely includes some steep pitches, but most of the big grunts are well into the ride. If you're a novice, Sweetwater will suit you nicely if you simply turn around and head back when things start getting nasty. For the rest of you, the trail becomes increasingly narrow and challenging as it heads to the eastern end of the lake near the Sweetwater River inflow.

As the trail leaves the reservoir area, it begins to follow the Sweetwater River northeast through land recently acquired by the U.S. Fish and Wildlife Service. Although there is trail on the ground through the Rancho San Diego area that ultimately connects to Campo Road (94), Fish and Wildlife has not yet determined if or how public access will be allowed. Tempting as it may be to try to make the connection, the ecologically sensitive area now managed by Fish and Wildlife should be avoided until a final public use determination has been made. Check with the agency before venturing upstream. The recommended ride has you turning around before you get into trouble.

Typical fence-line trail at Sweetwater Reservoir.

THE DRIVE

Take I-805 south to the E Street/Bonita Road exit. If you're coming south on I-5 instead, take I-54 east approximately two miles until it intersects I-805, then head south about a mile to the off ramp. Turn LEFT (east) onto Bonita Road. At 3.5 miles, Bonita Road takes a hard left at a traffic signal, but you will continue STRAIGHT through the light and onto San Miguel Road. Continue an additional 1.0 miles and turn LEFT on Summit Meadow Road. Continue to the top of the hill and park in the free day-use area just before the kiosk. The trailhead is just across the road toward the lake.

RIDE 10

SWEETWATER RESERVOIR

INCREMENTAL DISTANCE	CUMULATIVE DISTANCE	DESCRIPTION OF RIDE	DISTANCE TO FINISH
	0.0	Start measuring from the trailhead across from the day use parking area. You'll be heading EAST on rolling access road for the next mile.	7.2
	1.1	Bear RIGHT passing the kiosk on your left. The trail will narrow and begin rolling more steeply.	6.1
	1.9	Pass through the old gate and take either fork of the trail to the lookout on top of Cactus Hill.	5.3
2.3	2.3	Welcome to the Cactus Hill viewpoint. Continue along the fence line as the trail descends steeply.	4.9
	3.6	Welcome to the horse gate and the end of the singletrack. Until further notice, this is the designated turnaround point for the ride. Check with U.S. Fish and Wildlife before exploring further.	3.6
4.9	7.2	Back at the car.	0.0

MOUNTAINS

David Lehr climbs the Anderson Truck Trail above El Capitan Reservoir.

11 ANDERSON TRUCK TRAIL

ROUTE TYPE	Loop (or Out-n-Back)
DISTANCE	12.9 miles
RIDING TIME	3 hours
ELEVATION GAIN	1700 ft
AEROBIC SCALE	4/5
BURN FACTOR	3.5/5
SCARE-O-METER	2/5
LAND MANAGER	U.S. Forest Service - Cleveland National Forest - Descanso Ranger District
INFORMATION	619-445-6235

This ride provides an easily accessible and rewarding introduction to the enticing terrain that defines much of central San Diego County. The trail ascends north from the intersection of I-8 and Harbison Canyon Road, providing a great view of El Capitan Reservoir as the trail rises above Alpine into the thick chaparral of the Cleveland National Forest. Although the route involves quite a bit of climbing, the consistent grade and solid tread make this trail eminently rideable for all but the true novice. The trail's well-drained, semi-sandy soils also make this an excellent wet weather ride. The trail, particularly the upper half, offers little shade and can get quite warm in the summer months. Although you'll pass quite a few private garden hoses near the top of the ride, water is generally unavailable to the public until you get back down to Alpine.

As described below, the first 2/3 of the recommended loop has you climbing on dirt, followed by a fast, paved descent back to the car. Most of the climb follows an abandoned truck trail that has evolved almost entirely into singletrack. If you prefer, and you may, the ride can be done as an out-n-back to avoid the blacktop. If you decide to stick with the loop but would like to reverse directions in order to descend on the dirt, just keep a sharp eye out for weary uphillers, other trail users, and unsuspecting rattlesnakes. If you're thinking about doing the car shuttle to the top, think again you lazy lima bean.

THE DRIVE

From I-8 traveling east

Exit at Harbison Canyon/Dunbar Lane. Continue STRAIGHT off the ramp and onto Alpine Blvd. traveling east. Continue 1.0 miles to Peutz Valley Road. Turn LEFT and park under the highway overpass. Lock the car.

Anderson Truck Trail—Ride 11

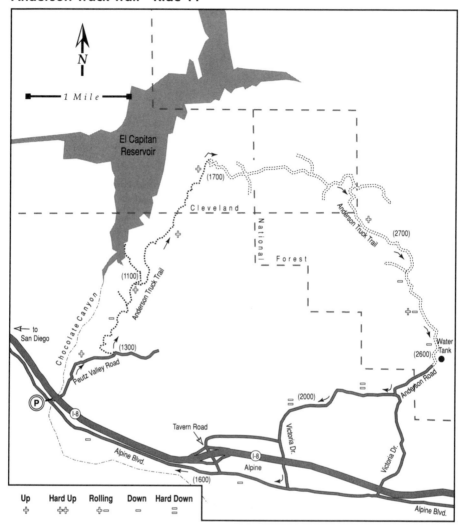

RIDE 11

ANDERSON TRUCK TRAIL

Incremental Distance	Cumulative Distance	Description of Ride	Distance to Finish
	0.0	Continue NORTH on the pavement of Peutz Valley Road toward El Capitan Reservoir.	12.9
0.8	0.8	Look for the unmarked but well-traveled singletrack trailhead on your left. You will descend toward El Capitan for several minutes before beginning the long climb.	12.1
0.7	1.5	Bear RIGHT at the Y	11.4
	1.8	Continue STRAIGHT on the main trail, but you may want to make note of the easy-to-miss singletrack beneath you to the left. It makes an out-n-back to the reservoir one mile away.	11.1
	3.7	The trail widens considerably as it switches back away from the reservoir.	9.2
	4.0	Pass the "Road Closed" barrier intended to keep vehicles approaching from the opposite direction off the section of trail you just covered. Beyond this point, the trail becomes much more of a dirt road and you may encounter an occasional motorized vehicle.	8.9
	4.1	Continue STRAIGHT through the 4-way-intersection to continue the climb on the main road.	8.9
4.3	5.2	Bear LEFT at the T.	8.7
	5.5	Pass the private driveway on the left.	7.4
0.4	5.6	Bear RIGHT. (left takes you to a private dead end)	7.3
	8.0	Pass the large water tower on your left and through the gate which is locked from sunset to sunrise. You will now be on the pavement of Anderson Road and the beginning of your descent to Alpine.	4.9
2.8	8.4	RIGHT on Victoria Drive.	4.5
2.0	10.4	RIGHT on Alpine Blvd.	2.5
2.5	12.9	RIGHT on Peutz Valley Road and back to the parking area.	0.0

12 LAGUNA MOUNTAINS

12a BIG LAGUNA TRAIL

ROUTE TYPE	Loop
DISTANCE	7.5 miles
RIDING TIME	1 hour
ELEVATION GAIN	500 ft
AEROBIC SCALE	2/5
BURN FACTOR	2/5
SCARE-O-METER	1.5/5
LAND MANAGER	U.S. Forest Service - Cleveland National Forest - Descanso Ranger District
INFORMATION	619-445-6235

If you're an expert, the Big Laguna Trail is the reason you're a mountain biker. If you're a novice, it's the reason you're about to become one. Although not an extreme challenge for lungs or legs, the rolling terrain and gorgeous vistas that define this inspirational ride make this relatively short loop one of San Diego's greatest pleasures. Other trail users feel the same, so expect to encounter others and, as always, be on your best behavior. It will be a sad day if the Big Laguna is ever closed to bikes. Don't let it happen.

Yuki Matsuura on the Big Laguna Trail.

Big Laguna Trail, Noble Canyon/Indian Creek Trail, Sheephead Mountain Road, Kitchen Creek/ Thing Valley Loop—Rides 12a, 12b, 12c, 12d

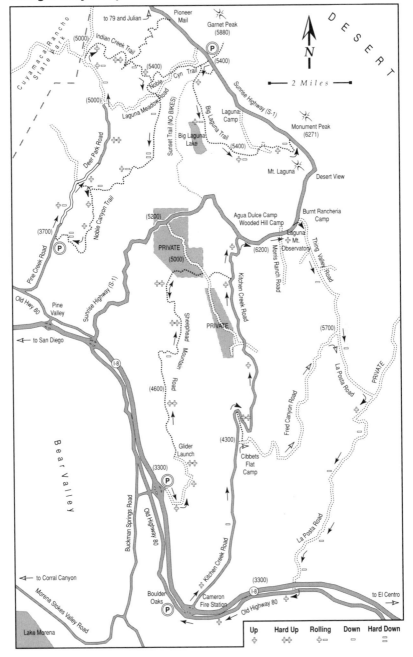

The loop described below is roughly 2/3 dirt (singletrack) and 1/3 Sunrise Highway. But if you prefer, you can turn it into a 100% dirt out-n-back by making the obvious adjustment to the directions below. Either way, you can't go wrong.

THE DRIVE

Take I-8 east just past Pine Valley and exit at Sunrise Highway. Turn LEFT (north) and follow the highway uphill into the Laguna Recreation Area of the Cleveland National Forest. Park at the generous turnout at the Noble Canyon Trailhead at mile 14 (just beyond mile marker 27.0). Park at the turnout and don't forget to display your National Forest Adventure Pass.

RIDE 12a

BIG LAGUNA TRAIL

Incremental Distance	Cumulative Distance	Description of Ride	Distance to Finish
	0.0	Start WEST on the Noble Canyon Trail, but start looking left for the Big Laguna Trail.	7.5
0.1	0.1	Turn LEFT off of Noble Canyon and onto the Big Laguna Trail heading south toward Big Laguna Lake.	7.4
	1.1	Pass the Sunset Trail on your right. NO BIKES.	6.4
	2.6	You've been following the eastern edge of Laguna Meadow. Follow the trail as it begins to veer away from the meadow, leaving Big Laguna Lake behind you.	4.9
2.8	2.9	Turn RIGHT, following the fence across the lumpy meadow. You'll soon pass the turnoff to Laguna Camp on your left. After crossing the meadow, your trail bears right into the tree line.	4.6
0.7	3.6	Cross the creek and bear LEFT up the canyon, through the gate and away from the meadow area.	3.9
	4.3	Cross the horse gate after the short steep climb.	3.2
0.9	4.5	Cross the dirt road twice and continue straight off the trail and onto the access road marked "Not a Through Road".	3.0
0.5	5.0	Turn LEFT off of the road and back onto the singletrack. It's well worn but not hard to miss. Enjoy the descent but watch out for other trail users.	2.5

| 0.4 | 5.4 | Turn LEFT onto Sunrise Highway and head back to the Noble Canyon trailhead parking area. | 2.1 |
| 2.1 | 7.5 | Back at the car. If you're feeling energetic, feel free to explore more of the Noble Canyon Trail where your ride started. | 0.0 |

12b NOBLE CANYON/INDIAN CREEK TRAIL

ROUTE TYPE	Loop
DISTANCE	17.3 miles
RIDING TIME	4 hours
ELEVATION GAIN	3000 ft
AEROBIC SCALE	5/5
BURN FACTOR	4/5
SCARE-O-METER	4/5
LAND MANAGER	U.S. Forest Service - Cleveland National Forest - Descanso Ranger District
INFORMATION	619-445-6235

You are about to embark on one of the world's great singletrack adventures. Snaking through the Laguna Mountains (close cousin of the nearby Cuyamacas), the Noble Canyon Trail will take you from pine forest to poison oak to prickly pear cactus. If your timing is right (early spring, perhaps), you can feel the cool crunch of snow under your tires and, an hour later, be peeling off clothes like a belly dancer as you pedal through the parched bottom section of this epic ride. Few trails can expose you to the kind of climatic and ecological diversity that defines the Noble Canyon experience. Camping is available along the trail, but you must first acquire a permit from the Forest Service.

The initial part of the ride does involve a bit of pavement, but you will leave the blacktop behind at mile 3.5 and be well on your way to the tight and lumpy Indian Creek singletrack. The remainder of the ride (over 12 miles) will be nearly pure singletrack all the way back to the car. Water is generally available at the upper trailhead at Sunrise Highway, but reaching it will take you approximately two miles further up the trail than the ride outlined below.

As something of a mecca for fat tire riders, the Noble Canyon Trail should be treated with the care and respect it deserves. Unfortunately, the trail's notoriety has made it something of a flashpoint for local trail conflict, and Forest Service managers are, understandably, keeping a close eye on the trail and its diverse group of users. The fact that the both ends of the trail are accessible by car has ensured high usage and has attracted quite a bit of one-way (downhill) bicycle use. The trail's narrow gauge and densely overgrown blind curves not only make it a joy to ride but also demand a degree of caution. As is the case on almost any public trail, you should expect to encounter horses, hikers, and mountain bikers traveling in both directions. Always yield trail.

THE DRIVE

Take I-8 east approximately 50 miles from SD and exit at Pine Valley. Turn LEFT at the bottom of the ramp and continue approximately 0.5 miles to Old Highway 80. Turn LEFT and continue west an additional 1.0 miles until you reach the Pine Creek bridge. Cross the bridge and immediately take a hard RIGHT turn onto Pine Creek Road. Continue an additional 1.5 miles to the Cleveland National Forest/Noble Canyon parking area. If the parking area immediately adjacent to the road is full (god forbid), you can turn RIGHT at the National Forest sign, cross the creek, and look for additional parking in the day use camping area. Remember, you'll need to display an annual or day use Adventure Pass on your vehicle to park anywhere within the National Forest boundary.

*Anne Carey of the U.S. Forest Service and Tom
Shjarback keep a close eye on the Noble Canyon Trail.*

RIDE 12b

NOBLE CANYON/INDIAN CREEK TRAIL

Incremental Distance	Cumulative Distance	Description of Ride	Distance to Finish
	0.0	Start measuring from the large Cleveland National Forest/Noble Canyon trail sign in the parking area. Continue NORTH on the pavement of Pine Creek Road. The road will roll and climb, culminating in a steep, paved pitch.	17.3
	3.5	Continue STRAIGHT across the cattle guard and onto the dirt downhill. Ignore Laguna Meadow Road ascending to the right.	13.8
	4.9	Pass the "Rockhouse" on your left and begin looking right for the Indian Creek Trail.	12.4
5.0	5.0	Cross the small, typically dry creek and immediately turn RIGHT onto the Indian Creek singletrack.	12.3
	5.3	Open (and close behind you) the barb wire fence. The trail continues uphill along the fence line.	12.0
	7.0	Continue STRAIGHT at the Champagne Pass intersection. Right turn option takes you to an out-n-back viewpoint. Left turn option connects to Pioneer Mail picnic area on Sunrise Highway.	10.3
	8.0	Cross the creek and begin climbing again on the singletrack on the opposite side of the meadow.	9.3
3.9	9.0	Join the Noble Canyon trail. Turn RIGHT (downhill) to begin the main descent. Left turn option takes you up Noble Canyon to Sunrise Highway and fresh water (approximately 2 miles).	8.3
	9.7	CROSS Laguna Meadow Road and continue downhill on the singletrack.	7.6
	10.1	Open (and close behind you) the trail gate.	7.2
	12.5	Bear RIGHT at the Y remaining on the singletrack.	4.8

continues

NOBLE CANYON/INDIAN CREEK TRAIL *(continued)*

INCREMENTAL DISTANCE	CUMULATIVE DISTANCE	DESCRIPTION OF RIDE	DISTANCE TO FINISH
5.3	14.2	Turn LEFT to remain on Noble Canyon Trail. Right turn option takes you back to Pine Creek Road in approximately 0.5 miles but avoids about 1.5 miles of additional climbing and descending on the Noble Canyon Trail.	3.1
	17.0	Arrive at the Noble Canyon day use area. Bear RIGHT on the pavement to return to the parking area on Pine Creek Road.	0.3
3.1	17.3	Back at the car.	0.0

Jon Purcell trying to keep up with Jonathan Purcell at the top of Noble Canyon.

12c SHEEPHEAD MOUNTAIN ROAD

ROUTE TYPE	Out-n-Back
DISTANCE	12.2 miles
RIDING TIME	3 hours
ELEVATION GAIN	2000 ft
AEROBIC SCALE	5/5
BURN FACTOR	5/5
SCARE-O-METER	3/5
LAND MANAGER	U.S. Forest Service - Cleveland National Forest - Descanso Ranger District
INFORMATION	619-445-6235

If you've ever exited I-8 east at Buckman Springs (perhaps on your way to ride number 14 in Corral Canyon), you may have glanced northeast across the highway and stared longingly at the road cut that traverses the hillside, eventually disappearing over the ridge. Well, here's your chance to put the mystery to rest. Sheephead Mountain Road was once capable of taking you all the way to Kitchen Creek Road and, ultimately, Sunrise Highway. Imagine how happy you'd be. Sheephead Mountain Road would still make the connection if not for the fact that just when you've gotten within spittin' distance of Kitchen Creek, the road runs into one of the many private inholdings within the Cleveland National Forest. To date, there is no legal easement or go-around that will allow you to make the connection without doing some pretty scary bush wacking—not recommended. By the time you've gotten to approximately mile 6, the road is beginning to skirt private property and, as indicated below, this is the recommended turnaround point. Tempting as it may be to continue, either by trespassing or wacking your way along the extremely messy chaparral superhighway, this is not the time to push the limits. This is the time, however, to get in touch with the Cleveland National Forest and/or your local trails group and let your trail brothers and sisters know that you'd like to volunteer to help make the connection.

Currently, the first three mile stretch of Sheephead Mountain Road rising from Buckman Springs is used quite regularly by hanglider and paraglider pilots who love to jump off the top of the hill. Clearly, they have gone insane. But you gotta love those guys and gals because they have contributed directly to the upkeep of the road. Beyond the first three miles, the road begins to disintegrate and, in fact, has been intentionally blown out in a few spots to discourage motorized vehicle traffic. On the accompanying map, the portion of the "road" beyond the glider launch is rough enough to qualify as "trail" according to the legend. All of this is good news for mountain bikers. Other than the glider pilots, the biggest group of trail users on Sheephead Mountain Road consists of undocumented immigrants attempting to walk around the I-8 immigration checkpoint near Buckman Springs. Feel free to pick up any garbage or stomp out any smoldering fires you may encounter.

The author climbs Sheephead Mountain Road into the Lagunas.

THE DRIVE

Take I-8 east and exit at Buckman Springs Road. Turn LEFT (east) at the bottom of the ramp and continue 0.25 miles, passing under the highway and past the rest area. The road quickly turns to dirt. Park in whatever shade you can find near the glider landing zone.

RIDE 12c

SHEEPHEAD MOUNTAIN ROAD

INCREMENTAL DISTANCE	CUMULATIVE DISTANCE	DESCRIPTION OF RIDE	DISTANCE TO FINISH
	0.0	Start pedaling SOUTH (feels like east) on the dirt. The road switches back to begin climbing NORTH (feels like west).	12.2
	1.5	Crest the ridge and pass the access road descending on your right (you may want to check it out later). You will continue to climb	10.7

		along the ridge, admiring Horse Canyon on your right.	
	2.7	Pass the glider launch on your left, admiring the crazy people. The road gets rougher from here on out.	9.5
	3.4	Follow the short descent toward the canyon, then resume climbing on the narrow and loose.	8.8
6.1	6.1	The road/trail reaches something of a T. Private property, confusion and possible arrest lay ahead. Head back the way you came up.	6.1
12.2	12.2	Back at the car.	0.0

12d KITCHEN CREEK/THING VALLEY LOOP

ROUTE TYPE	Loop
DISTANCE	28.7 miles
RIDING TIME	4-5 hours
ELEVATION GAIN	3100 ft
AEROBIC SCALE	5/5
BURN FACTOR	3/5 (5/5 if you do it in reverse)
SCARE-O-METER	3/5
LAND MANAGER	U.S. Forest Service - Cleveland National Forest - Descanso Ranger District
INFORMATION	619-445-6235

Here's one for the lungs. 1700 feet of nearly unbroken climbing will earn you a good night's rest. Although nearly all the climbing is paved, the mountainous vistas and dirty, loose descent definitely qualify this as a worthwhile mountain bike ride. The recommended direction of travel is up on the blacktop and down on the dirt, but you can certainly reverse the description below or, if you dare, turn the whole thing into a 100% dirt out-n-back on Thing Valley/La Post Road. Just keep in mind you'll probably be doubling the calories and adding at least 50% to the total ride time.

The ride is fairly straight forward with the exception of one major option that, if you choose, will bisect the described loop and take you on the very attractive Fred Canyon Road either on the way up or the way down. There is a bit of potential confusion to watch out for as Thing Valley Road, as it is referred to off of Sunrise Highway, quietly evolves into La Posta Road as it descends. "Thing Valley Road" is probably something of a misnomer, and you may see a sign change sometime in the future turning the whole length into "La Posta".

THE DRIVE

Take I-8 east and exit at Kitchen Creek Road, approximately 10 miles southeast of Pine Valley. Old Highway 80 is immediately to your Right. Park wherever you can. The measured ride begins from the intersection of Kitchen Creek Road and Old Highway 80.

RIDE 12d

KITCHEN CREEK/THING VALLEY LOOP

Incremental Distance	Cumulative Distance	Description of Ride	Distance to Finis
	0.0	Start NORTH on the pavement of Kitchen Creek Road.	28.7
	2.4	Cross the Pacific Crest Trail. NO BIKES.	26.3
	2.7	After a brief descent, cross the bridge over Kitchen Creek.	26.0
4.8	4.8	Welcome to Cibbets Flat Camp. You can continue climbing on the pavement of Kitchen Creek or, better yet, turn RIGHT into Cibbets Flat Camp and immediately LEFT, crossing the stone footbridge and onto the dirt parallel to the road.	23.9
0.8	5.6	If you took the recommended dirt option mentioned above, you will now rejoin the pavement of Kitchen Creek Road as it makes a hairpin turn temporarily to the right (south) before continuing to climb. The road is still paved but less so.	23.1
	10.4	Pass a gated, dirt access road on your left. This is actually the end of Sheephead Mountain Road rising up from I-8 at Buckman Springs. Unfortunately it doesn't descend further than about a mile before forcing you into a pickle surrounded by private property. Worth a brief look but nothing more than an out-n-back at this time.	18.3
6.4	12.0	RIGHT on Sunrise Highway. Continue east on the road shoulder 1.9 miles.	16.7
1.9	13.9	RIGHT on Thing Valley Road (also called La Posta Road or La Posta Truck Trail).	14.8
	14.5	STRAIGHT at the T.	14.2

	15.2	Cross the Pacific Crest Trail. NO BIKES.	13.5
	16.2	Pass several structures on your left. Stay off of anything that smells like private property.	12.5
	17.5	Pass Fred Canyon Road on your right. (Fred Canyon Road is a nice option that would take you back down through Cibbets Flat.) From here on down, the road is referred to as La Posta Road or La Posta Truck Trail.	11.2
	19.4	Pass through the lower Forest Service gate.	9.3
5.6	19.5	Turn RIGHT to remain on La Posta Road. Left is gated, private Indian land.	9.2
	22.3	Through another gate.	6.4
	23.2	Thing Ranch Road joins La Posta Road from the left. Continue south.	5.5
	25.2	Continue south across the private parcel, following the road easement.	3.5
6.3	25.8	Pass under I-8 and turn RIGHT (west) on Old Highway 80.	2.9
2.9	28.7	Back at the car.	0.0

13 CUYAMACA RANCHO STATE PARK

Less than an hour from San Diego, Cuyamaca Rancho State Park offers some of the most beautiful and easily accessible hiking, bicycling, and horseback riding in the county. Boasting more than 30,000 total acres and nearly 110 miles of trail and fire road (not all open to bikes), the park is a popular destination for outdoor enthusiasts of every persuasion.

For more than 7,000 years, the Cuyamaca Mountains have been a summertime escape from the hot weather of the lowlands. Local natives frequented the relatively wet and cool Cuyamacas, leaving a rich collection of archaeological sites before being crowded out by the arrival of Europeans in the mid-1800s. A brief gold rush, beginning in 1860, further displaced the native population, and much of the area spent the next 50 years or so as ranchland under a series of private owners. The land was purchased by the state in 1933 and has since grown into one of the California's largest parks.

In 1988, just as mountain biking began its rapid rise in popularity, California State Parks adopted a "Trails Closed/Fire Roads Open" policy with regard to bicycle use. The result, of course, was the immediate exclusion of bicycles from trails they had been sharing with other users for several years. In fact, it was this particular policy that was largely responsible for launching the grassroots

East Side Trail at Cuyamaca Rancho State Park.

mountain bike advocacy and trails access movement nationwide. When riding in any California State Park, including Cuyamaca Rancho, you should assume that all trails (defined as 60 inches wide or less) are closed unless specifically posted "open" to bicycles. Fire roads (wider than 60 inches) should be considered open unless specifically posted "closed." Although local park managers have the authority to make decisions about opening and closing specific trails, most land managers have been reluctant to do anything that might seem to depart from the restrictive sentiments expressed in Sacramento. As a result, few trails (typically referred to as "singletrack" by bicyclists) are open anywhere in the California State Park System.

The good news in Cuyamaca Rancho is the fact that bicyclists currently do have access to over 65 miles of the park's total 110 miles of trail and fire road, including several modest but precious stretches of relatively narrow trail that would otherwise be off limits to bicycle use. The Oakzanita Trail, parts of East Mesa Fire Road near the connection to Deer Park Road, and the very recently opened East Side Trail from East Mesa Fire Road to the Sweetwater River staging area, are exactly the type of narrow, shared-use trail that mountain bikers would like to see more of. But that will only come about if we mountain bikers continue to demonstrate our commitment to responsible riding by working closely with local land managers and other trail users to protect the precious trails we all love.

13a GRAND LOOP

ROUTE TYPE	Loop
DISTANCE	16.5 miles
RIDING TIME	2.5 hours
ELEVATION GAIN	2000 ft
AEROBIC SCALE	3.5/5
BURN FACTOR	2.5/5
SCARE-O-METER	2/5
LAND MANAGER	State of California Department of Parks and Recreation
INFORMATION	760-765-0755

You're gonna like this one for sure. Much of what has made the Cuyamacas such a popular outdoor destination is captured in the following ride. You'll rise and fall through open meadow, oak grove and pine forest that will almost make you forget the burning in your legs. The recommended route puts you on lots of access road (some of it quite narrow, rough, and satisfying) and a bit of pavement, including a couple of minutes on Highway 79 as you cross to the west side of the park. Watch out for other trail users and keep an eye peeled for mountain lions lest they peel you.

THE DRIVE

Take I-8 east and exit at Highway 79 towards Julian. Turn LEFT (north) and continue an additional 3.0 miles. Turn LEFT (still Highway 79) following the signs to Cuyamaca Rancho State Park/Julian. Continue 5.5 miles and turn RIGHT onto Park Headquarters Road. There will be a small parking area immediately in front of you near the highway. You may park here for free or continue on Headquarters Road to the pay parking area. Alternately, you can get back on Highway 79 and park back at the Sweetwater River staging area. The measured ride begins on Green Valley Fire Road just below Park Headquarters.

Grand Loop—Ride 13a

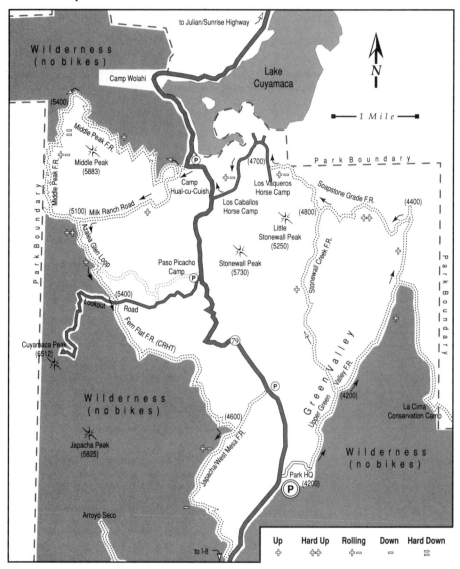

RIDE 13a

GRAND LOOP

INCREMENTAL DISTANCE	CUMULATIVE DISTANCE	DESCRIPTION OF RIDE	DISTANCE TO FINISH
	0.0	Wherever you managed to park, make your way to Green Valley Fire Road, between Park Headquarters and the Sweetwater River. Start measuring from the motorized vehicle boundary gate on Green Valley Fire Road at the north end of Camp Cuyamaca.	16.5
	0.4	Continue STRAIGHT past the Cold Stream Trail on your left.	16.2
	0.8	Continue STRAIGHT past the Harvey Moore Trail on your right.	15.8
	0.9	Bear RIGHT to remain on the Green Valley Fire Road. Left turn option takes you to Stonewall Peak, which is well worth exploring next time.	15.7
	2.4	Continue on Green Valley Fire Road, passing the turnoff to La Cima Conservation Camp on your right.	14.2
3.1	3.1	LEFT on Soapstone Grade Road.	13.4
	3.9	Cross the saddle and begin descending.	12.6
1.7	4.8	RIGHT at the T onto Stonewall Peak Fire Road and descend through the meadow.	11.7
1.0	5.8	RIGHT onto the pavement of Los Vaqueros Road.	10.7
0.4	6.2	LEFT at the gate.	10.3
	6.8	Pass Los Vaqueros Horse Camp on your left.	9.7
0.9	7.1	RIGHT (north) onto Highway 79.	9.5
0.5	7.6	As Highway 79 curves right, bear LEFT off the highway toward Hual-Cu-Cuish Boy Scout Camp. Leave the pavement and pass through the gate onto Milk Ranch Road. The Boy Scout camp will be to your left. Begin climbing.	8.9
	7.9	Straight past the Middle Peak Fire Road on your right. Consider the Middle Peak loop trail for next time. It will add approximately 2.2 miles to the overall ride.	8.7

continues

GRAND LOOP *(continued)*

INCREMENTAL DISTANCE	CUMULATIVE DISTANCE	DESCRIPTION OF RIDE	DISTANCE TO FINISH
1.7	9.3	LEFT on Azalea Glen Loop Trail toward Azalea Spring.	7.2
	9.6	STRAIGHT toward Azalea Spring, passing the Conejos Trail on your right.	7.0
	10.0	Pass the California Riding and Hiking Trail to your left.	6.5
0.8	10.1	Bear RIGHT above Azalea Spring onto the California Riding and Hiking Trail.	6.4
0.6	10.7	Turn RIGHT onto the pavement of Lookout Road and immediately LEFT to continue on the California Riding and Hiking Trail (also referred to at this point as Fern Flat). Follow the sign toward Arroyo Seco Trail Camp.	5.9
	12.5	Pass the connector to the California Riding and Hiking Trail to your right.	4.1
	12.9	Pass the West Mesa Trail connector to your right.	3.7
2.6	13.3	RIGHT on Japacha Fire Road.	3.2
0.7	14.0	Bear LEFT, avoiding the wilderness area to the right.	2.6
	15.2	Pass the West Side Trail to your left.	1.3
1.4	15.4	Bear LEFT and drop down to Highway 79. Turn LEFT again onto the pavement and follow the road back to Park Headquarters.	1.1
1.1	16.5	Back at the car.	0.0

13b OAKZANITA PEAK

ROUTE TYPE	Out-n-Back
DISTANCE	8.7 miles
RIDING TIME	1.0 hours
ELEVATION GAIN	1100 ft
AEROBIC SCALE	3/5
BURN FACTOR	3/5
SCARE-O-METER	2/5
LAND MANAGER	State of California Department of Parks and Recreation
INFORMATION	760-765-0755

Oakzanita Peak—Ride 13b

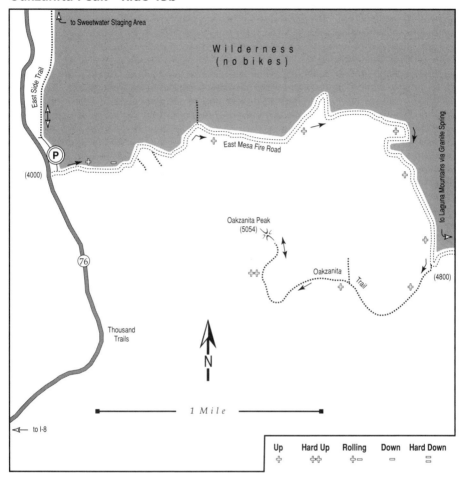

This experience takes you along the southern boundary of the park on the consistent but occasionally bumpy East Mesa Fire Road. The challenge of this ride suits both novices and experts and offers the reward of beautiful Oakzanita Peak and a nice downhill to finish up. With the exception of the technical singletrack that makes up the final pitch to the peak, it's all access road.

THE DRIVE

Follow the general directions outlined above and park at the East Mesa Fire Road trailhead approximately 1.0 miles north of the southern park boundary, just past mile marker 3.5.

RIDE 13b

OAKZANITA PEAK

INCREMENTAL DISTANCE	CUMULATIVE DISTANCE	DESCRIPTION OF RIDE	DISTANCE TO FINISH
	0.0	Start from the East Mesa Fire Road trailhead. Cross the locked gate and begin climbing EAST on the fire road.	8.7
2.9	2.9	Turn RIGHT onto the Oakzanita singletrack trail.	5.8
0.8	3.7	Turn LEFT toward Oakzanita Peak and continue to climb on the increasingly technical singletrack.	4.9
0.6	4.3	Welcome to Oakzanita Peak. Return the way you came.	4.3
4.3	8.7	Back at the car.	0.0

13c BOULDER CREEK LOOP DELUXE

ROUTE TYPE	Loop
DISTANCE	42.1 miles
RIDING TIME	5-6 hours
ELEVATION GAIN	4000 ft
AEROBIC SCALE	5/5
BURN FACTOR	3/5
SCARE-O-METER	2/5
LAND MANAGER	U.S. Forest Service - Cleveland National Forest - Descanso Ranger District State of California Department of Parks and Recreation
INFORMATION	619-445-6235 (Cleveland National Forest) or 760-765-0755 (State Parks)

Cuyamaca Rancho State Park is but one way to experience the Cuyamaca Mountains. If you'd like see the Cuyamacas from all angles, and you've got a few hours to kill, then the following odyssey is a highly recommended tour of San Diego County's wild center. You'll not only spend time on some of the more familiar trails of the state park east of Cuyamaca Peak, but you will also see your favorite hilltops from the drier, less-traveled western perspective. Although a good portion of this ride is on dirt or paved road where you may encounter an occasional passenger vehicle, don't despair; this is definitely a mountain bike ride you'll not soon forget. Bring water, sunscreen, and an extra lung.

You'll spend some time on pavement and a lot of time on dirt access road, some of which, particularly within the State Park, is plenty technical. After start-

Boulder Creek Loop Deluxe—Ride 13c

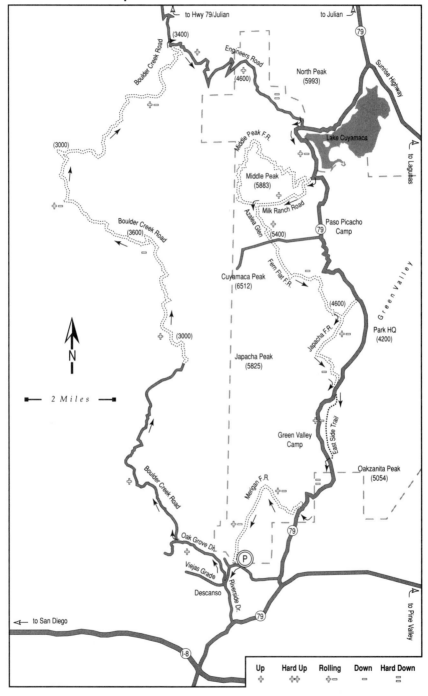

to Hwy 79/Julian

to Julian

79

(3400)

Boulder Creek Road

Engineers Road

(4600)

North Peak
(5993)

Sunrise Highway

to Lagunas

(3000)

Lake Cuyamaca

Middle Peak F.R.

Middle Peak
(5883)

Azalea Glen

Milk Ranch Road

Boulder Creek Road
(3600)

Paso Picacho
Camp

79

Green Valley

Cuyamaca Peak
(6512)

Fern Flat F.R.

(4600)

Park HQ
(4200)

(5400)

N

(3000)

Japacha Peak
(5825)

Japacha F.R.

2 Miles

Green Valley
Camp

East Side Trail

Oakzanita Peak
(5054)

Boulder Creek Road

Merigan F.R.

79

Oak Grove Dr.

P

Viejas Grade

Riverside Dr.

Descanso

79

to San Diego

I-8

to Pine Valley

Up	Hard Up	Rolling	Down	Hard Down

ing out, you may not see easily accessible drinking water for many miles. So bring plenty and pack a lunch.

THE DRIVE

Take I-8 east and exit at Highway 79 toward Julian. Turn LEFT (north) at the bottom of the ramp and continue 1.5 miles to Riverside Drive. Turn LEFT on Riverside Drive and continue an additional 1.0 miles to the small state park parking area just past Merigan Ranch and adjacent to Holidays On Horseback. Park here, apply fresh lube, and check your water supply. You'll be returning to the parking lot via the Merigan Fire Road in 5–6 hours. Giddy up.

RIDE 13c

BOULDER CREEK LOOP DELUXE

INCREMENTAL DISTANCE	CUMULATIVE DISTANCE	DESCRIPTION OF RIDE	DISTANCE TO FINISH
	0.0	Start measuring from the parking area. Head SOUTH back down Riverside Drive toward Highway 79.	42.1
0.6	0.6	Turn RIGHT on Viejas Grade and immediately RIGHT again onto Oak Grove Drive.	41.5
1.6	2.2	Turn RIGHT on Boulder Creek Road.	39.9
	3.9	Cross your first cattle guard as you enter the Cleveland National Forest.	38.2
5.1	7.3	Boulder Creek Road now becomes dirt. Continue climbing for another 2 miles before beginning the long decent to the creek bottom. You'll be passing the seldom seen "back side" of Cuyamaca Peak on your right.	34.8
	13.0	Cross Boulder Creek and continue on Boulder Creek Road as it rolls north.	29.1
13.0	20.3	Turn RIGHT on the pavement of Engineers Road, away from the Pine Hills Fire Station west of the intersection. Straight would take you to Julian via the paved continuation of Boulder Creek Road and Highway 79. You will now be climbing east on Engineers Road toward North Peak.	21.8
5.8	26.1	Turn RIGHT on Highway 79 to go around Lake Cuyamaca counterclockwise, eventually heading south. Refreshments are available in about a mile. If you're feeling pooped, you can take	16.0

		Highway 79 south all the way out of the park and back to the car in Descanso.	
1.4	27.5	Turn RIGHT onto the dirt of Milk Ranch Road as it passes the Hual-Cu-Cuish camp. Begin climbing with Middle Peak to your right. If you're feeling particularly energetic, you can throw in the Middle Peak Fire Road loop by turning right off of Milk Ranch Road. This option will add approximately 2.2 miles to your ride.	14.6
1.7	29.2	LEFT on Azalea Glen Loop Trail toward Azalea Spring.	12.9
	29.5	STRAIGHT toward Azalea Spring, passing the Conejos Trail on your right.	12.6
	29.9	Pass the California Riding and Hiking Trail to your left.	12.2
0.9	30.1	Bear RIGHT above Azalea Spring onto the California Riding and Hiking Trail.	12.0
0.6	30.7	Turn RIGHT onto the pavement of Lookout Road and immediately LEFT to continue on the California Riding and Hiking Trail (also referred to at this point as Fern Flat Fire Road). Follow the sign toward Arroyo Seco Trail Camp.	11.4
	32.5	Pass the connector to the California Riding and Hiking Trail to your right.	9.6
	32.9	Pass the West Mesa Trail connector to your right.	9.2
2.7	33.4	RIGHT on Japacha Fire Road.	8.7
0.6	34.0	Bear LEFT, avoiding the Wilderness area to the right.	8.1
	35.2	Pass the West Side Trail to your left.	6.9
1.3	35.3	Bear LEFT and drop down to Highway 79. Turn RIGHT onto the pavement and follow the Highway south 1/4 mile to the Sweetwater Staging Area on the left.	6.8
0.2	35.5	Take the Harvey Moore trail heading east from the Sweetwater Staging Area and continue up the hill a short distance until you encounter the start of the East Side Trail. Turn RIGHT onto the singletrack - one of the few trails currently open to bikes. Behave well or lose it.	6.6
1.4	36.9	The East Side Trail ends at the intersection of Highway 79 and the bottom of the East Mesa Fire Road. Bear LEFT (south) on Highway 79	5.2

continues

BOULDER CREEK LOOP DELUXE *(continued)*

INCREMENTAL DISTANCE	CUMULATIVE DISTANCE	DESCRIPTION OF RIDE	DISTANCE TO FINISH
		and begin descending. As you ride through the fast S turn section, keep a sharp eye peeled for the turnoff to the Merigan Fire Road on your right. It's very easy to miss, particularly if you're concentrating on not getting smeared by tourist traffic on the highway.	
2.0	38.9	Turn RIGHT on Merigan Fire Road. The next 3 miles of rolling trail see heavy equestrian use coming up from Descanso. Take it easy.	3.2
	40.1	Bear LEFT to stay on Merigan Fire Road.	2.0
3.2	42.1	Back at the car.	0.0

14 LAKE MORENA/CORRAL CANYON

ROUTE TYPE	Loop
DISTANCE	15.1 miles
RIDING TIME	2.5 hours
ELEVATION GAIN	2200 ft
AEROBIC SCALE	4/5
BURN FACTOR	4/5
SCARE-O-METER	3.5/5
LAND MANAGER	Corral Canyon - U.S. Forest Service, Cleveland National Forest - Descanso Ranger District Lake Morena - County of San Diego Department of Parks and Recreation
INFORMATION	619-445-6235 (Cleveland National Forest) or 619-694-4039 (County Parks)

If you've never visited the Lake Morena/Corral Canyon area, you're in for a pleasant surprise. Awaiting you is an extensive network of narrow trail and challenging fire road crisscrossing thousands of acres of dense chaparral, oak grove, rock, and boulder. Most of the riding in this area is a bit much for the novice, but more experienced and expert riders will find it challenging and inspirational. Corral Canyon is one of the county's few designated Off Highway Vehicle areas and should be ridden cautiously and with consideration for the motorized folks who have few other places in the county where they can legally recreate. Although your encounters with motorized users are likely to be few, don't forget that the folks with motors can't hear you coming. Stay alert, steer clear, and don't

Lake Morena/Corral Canyon—Ride 14

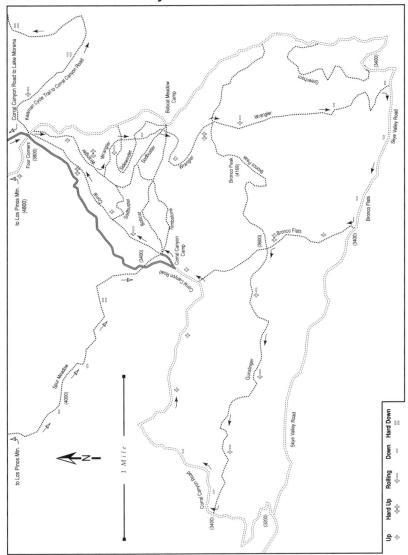

expect anyone with a motor to yield trail. They may never even notice you cling-
ing to the sumac on the side of the trail as they pass you by.

The recommended ride starts at the intersection of the Kearnan Cycle Trail
and Corral Canyon Road. But if roadside parking is a problem, or you'd like a

longer warm-up before hitting the dirt, you can also start from the Northshore Primitive Camping Area down by Lake Morena. It is also possible to drive all the way to Four Corners but that will deprive you of the opportunity to finish the ride with the positively sublime experience of descending on the Kearnan Cycle Trail. Aside from the initial paved climb to Four Corners, the ride described below is mostly singletrack with a bit of dirt road mixed in. Water is available mid-ride at the camping facilities, but you should be as self-sufficient as possible. Once you get going, it's very tempting to just keep exploring the intricacies of the Corral Canyon trail system. Go for it. Trail maps are posted intermittently at trail heads and camping areas.

THE DRIVE

Take I-8 east approximately 50 miles from San Diego. Exit at Buckman Springs. Turn RIGHT at the bottom of the ramp and continue 3.1 miles. Turn RIGHT at Morena Stokes Valley Road (follow the sign to Corral Canyon Off-Road Vehicle Area). Continue an additional 3.3 miles, passing Morena Reservoir on your left. Park where the Kearnan Cycle Trail intersects Corral Canyon Road.

RIDE 14

LAKE MORENA/CORRAL CANYON

INCREMENTAL DISTANCE	CUMULATIVE DISTANCE	DESCRIPTION OF RIDE	DISTANCE TO FINISH
	0.0	Begin measuring at the base of the Kearnan Cycle Trail by continuing WEST and ascending on the pavement of Corral Canyon Road.	15.1
2.3	2.3	Welcome to Four Corners and the start of the singletrack. Take Trail No. 1 ("Wrangler") on the opposite side of the dirt parking area.	12.8
	3.3	You will be riding over a large granite slab. Trail No. 1 continues from the uphill side of the slab.	11.8
	3.5	Continue STRAIGHT at the intersection.	11.6
	3.6	At the three-way fork continue STRAIGHT (middle fork).	11.5
	3.8	Continue STRAIGHT at the intersection. (Bobcat Meadow Camping Area will be immediately to your left across the road)	11.3
	4.3	Continue STRAIGHT (middle trail).	10.8
2.8	5.1	LEFT at the granite slab.	10.0

0.1	5.2	Bear RIGHT on the granite slab.	9.9
0.8	6.0	Turn RIGHT onto Skye Valley Road (a.k.a. Bronco Flats Loop)	9.1
0.7	6.7	Turn RIGHT onto Trail No. 5 ("Bronco Flats")	8.4
0.8	7.5	Bear LEFT at the intersection onto Trail No. 11 ("Gun Slinger")	7.6
1.8	9.3	Turn RIGHT onto Corral Canyon Road. If you're feeling tired or you've had enough singletrack, Corral Canyon Road can be ridden all the way back to Four Corners (about 3 miles).	5.8
1.8	11.1	Turn RIGHT across the cattle guard into Corral Canyon Camping Area. At the far end of the camp look for the Trail No. 2 ("Corral"), which continues up the canyon parallel to Corral Canyon Road.	4.0
1.3	12.4	Welcome back to Four Corners. Look for the Kearnan Cycle Trail which will take you right to your vehicle via one of San Diego's best downhills.	2.7
2.7	15.1	Welcome back to the parking area.	0.0

15 PALOMAR MOUNTAIN

15a WEST SIDE–NATE HARRISON GRADE

ROUTE TYPE	Loop
DISTANCE	40.8 miles
RIDING TIME	4 hours
ELEVATION GAIN	4500 ft
AEROBIC SCALE	5/5
BURN FACTOR	3/5
SCARE-O-METER	2/5
LAND MANAGER	U.S. Forest Service, Cleveland National Forest, Palomar Ranger District State of California Department of Parks and Recreation (Palomar Mountain State Park)
INFORMATION	760-788-0250 (Cleveland National Forest) and 760-742-3462 (Palomar Mountain State Park)

Why? Because it's there. Palomar Mountain rises from Pauma Valley like a rocket. You, unfortunately, will not rise like a rocket as you slowly grind your

West Side–Nate Harrison Grade, East Side—Rides 15a, 15b

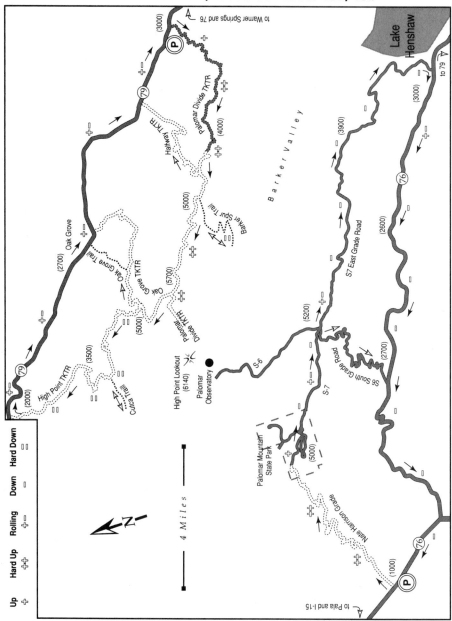

way up the Nate Harrison Grade on the western face of this punishing but rewarding resumé builder. Aside from the great view of northern San Diego County on the way up, the thing that makes this otherwise dry, exposed, and sometimes dusty ride worthwhile is the prize awaiting you at the top. Just when you think you've had about enough sun and thighburn, you'll find yourself emerging into the cool, lush forest of Palomar Mountain State Park. Unfortunately, none of the park's several miles of beautiful singletrack trail are open to bicycles. But you may want to rest up by taking a stroll through the one of the park's life-affirming groves of oak, pine, cedar, fir, and flowering shrub.

Unless you want to turn around and return via the same dirt road that got you to the top, the only descents available to you are paved. Both S-6 and S-7 will send you back down to Highway 76 on the blacktop and then return you to the bottom of the Nate Harrison on a mostly downhill cruise. The long way via S-7 is the route described below but if it sounds like too much of a road ride for your dirt-lovin' heart, S-6 will shave a dozen or so miles off of this otherwise 41 mile loop. If you're doing Palomar on a weekend, keep an eye peeled and an ear open for motorcycle riders who like to use S-7 as a racecourse.

THE DRIVE

Take I-15 north just past Escondido and exit at Highway 76 heading east toward Pala. Continue approximately 12.8 miles and look for Nate Harrison Road on your left as it disappears into the citrus groves. Look for parking near the intersection, but stay off private property. Don't pick fruit. The measured ride starts from the intersection of Highway 76 and Nate Harrison Road.

RIDE 15a

WEST SIDE–NATE HARRISON GRADE

Incremental Distance	Cumulative Distance	Description of Ride	Distance to Finish
	0.0	Start uphill on the pavement of Nate Harrison Road.	40.8
1.2	1.2	Pavement ends. Keep on climbin'.	39.6
6.7	7.9	Enter Palomar Mountain State Park.	32.9
0.3	8.2	Pavement starts. Keep on climbin'.	32.6
1.3	9.5	Arrive at the 5-way paved intersection. You'll be turning LEFT (not hard left) toward the ranger house, past park headquarters, and exiting the park onto S-7. Boucher Lookout Loop is worth the 1.5 mile round trip and you may also want to take the 3.4 mile loop down through the camp area to check out the facilities.	31.3

continues

WEST SIDE–NATE HARRISON GRADE *(continued)*

Incremental Distance	Cumulative Distance	Description of Ride	Distance to Finish
3.3	12.8	At the intersection with S-6, follow the signs to remain on S-7. If you're pooped or aren't looking for a long road ride, S-6 to your right will drop you back down to 76.	28.0
10.7	23.5	Turn RIGHT on 76 and begin the long but mostly downhill road ride back to Nate Harrison.	17.3
17.3	40.8	Back at the car.	0.0

15b EAST SIDE

Route Type	Loop
Distance	36.2 miles
Riding Time	All Day
Elevation Gain	5500 ft
Aerobic Scale	5/5
Burn Factor	3/5
Scare-o-meter	3/5
Land Manager	U.S. Forest Service, Cleveland National Forest, Palomar Ranger District
Information	760-788-0250

If the Nate Harrison Grade didn't give you the burn you're looking for, the east face of Palomar will. Hot, dry, and exposed, you'll find little relief along most of this 36 mile grunt. Although the ride described below takes you through a full-length loop, you should feel free to shorten the course as you see fit. Keep in mind that even after you've conquered the long but semi-steep dirt climb and descent, you'll still have a substantial road ride ahead of you to get back to the car. Fortunately some services are available on Highway 79. The Palomar Divide, Oak Grove, and High Point Truck Trails are, as their names imply, open to motorized vehicles, but you are unlikely see anyone other than your own riding buddies.

THE DRIVE

By hook or crook, get yourself to Highway 79 north of Warner Springs. The start of the Palomar Divide Truck Trail (Road number 9S07) is approximately 5 miles north of Warner Springs, just south of the 42.0 mile marker. You can probably park just outside the national forest boundary. Otherwise your vehicle will need to display a valid Adventure Pass.

RIDE 15b

EAST SIDE

INCREMENTAL DISTANCE	CUMULATIVE DISTANCE	DESCRIPTION OF RIDE	DISTANCE TO FINISH
	0.0	Start riding uphill from the bottom of the Palomar Divide Truck Trail at Highway 79.	36.2
	1.6	Enter the Cleveland National Forest. You'll be on an improved road for the next 5 miles.	34.6
6.1	6.1	Dirt begins.	30.1
	7.3	Continue STRAIGHT past the Halfway Truck Trail (road number 9S06) on your right.	28.9
	8.0	Continue STRAIGHT past the Barker Spur Trail on your left. However, if you are feeling very, very fresh and have lots of water, the 7.0 mile singletrack round trip down into Barker Canyon is a real treat. Theoretically, the Barker Spur Trail actually makes a loop that will ultimately bring you back to the High Point Truck Trail several miles further up the road, near the Oak Grove intersection. However, although the descent into Barker Valley is well established, the climb back out is much more tentative. Unless you are very fit, confident, and experienced, the Barker Spur Trail is best treated as an out-n-back. Mileages listed below do not include this detour.	28.2
5.6	11.7	Bear RIGHT at the Y and descend through the trees (you are now on the Oak Grove Truck Trail).	24.5
	11.8	Continue STRAIGHT onto Oak Grove Truck Trail (road number 9S09).	24.4
1.9	13.6	Turn LEFT onto High Point Truck Trail (road number 8S05)	22.6
	17.5	PASS the Cutca Trail on your left. The Cutca is rideable but eventually deadends at the Agua Tibia Wilderness (no bikes).	18.7
	19.9	Exit the Cleveland National Forest.	16.3
9.0	22.6	CROSS the sandy bed of Temecula Creek and continue STRAIGHT onto the pavement.	13.6
0.4	23.0	Turn RIGHT onto Highway 79 and begin the long grind southeast back into San Diego County.	13.2
13.2	36.2	Back at the car.	0.0

Palomar Divide Road descending toward Warner Springs.

16 INDIAN FLATS

ROUTE TYPE	Loop
DISTANCE	24.8 miles
RIDING TIME	4 Hours
ELEVATION GAIN	2000 ft
AEROBIC SCALE	5/5
BURN FACTOR	2/5
SCARE-O-METER	2/5
LAND MANAGER	U.S. Forest Service–Cleveland National Forest–Palomar Ranger District
INFORMATION	760-788-0250

The Indian Flats loop is a somewhat gentler and kinder version of the death march you may have already experienced on the east face of Palomar Mountain. Despite the fact that Indian Flats may be bit warmer in the afternoon due to the largely western exposure, the ride is definitely shorter and less harsh overall than Palomar. The middle third of the ride also offers a great rock garden tour as you pedal past the vast fields of sandstone polyps that seem to watch you go by like curious aliens. Getting there does require several miles of climbing on "pavement," but the road grade and terrain are certainly rough enough to qualify as a mountain bike ride.

THE DRIVE

Once again, get yourself to Highway 79 north of Warner Springs. Lost Valley Road (Road number 9S05) is approximately 1.5 miles north of Warner Springs. Park off of 79 near the Lost Valley Road intersection.

RIDE 16

INDIAN FLATS

Incremental Distance	Cumulative Distance	Description of Ride	Distance to Finish
	0.0	Start uphill (north) on the pavement of Lost Valley Road away from Highway 79.	24.8
	1.5	Enter the Cleveland National Forest.	23.3
6.7	6.7	Bear RIGHT onto the dirt past Indian Flats Campground on your left. If necessary, take the short detour down to the camp to water up.	18.1
	8.4	Leave Cleveland National Forest.	16.4
3.6	10.3	Turn RIGHT. Forest service road on Left dead-ends at private property.	14.5
1.0	11.3	Turn LEFT onto the pavement of Chihuahua Valley Road.	13.5
4.4	15.7	Turn LEFT onto Highway 79.	9.1
9.1	24.8	Back at the car.	0.0

Indian Flats—Ride 16

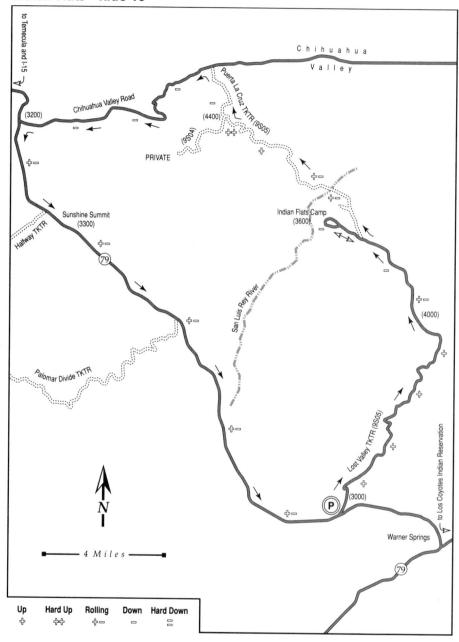

to Temecula and I-15

Chihuahua Valley

Puerta La Cruz TKTR (9S05)

Chihuahua Valley Road

(3200)

(4400)

(9S04)

PRIVATE

Sunshine Summit (3300)

Indian Flats Camp (3600)

Halfway TKTR

79

San Luis Rey River

(4000)

Palomar Divide TKTR

Lost Valley TKTR (9S05)

to Los Coyotes Indian Reservation

N

4 Miles

P

(3000)

Warner Springs

79

Up	Hard Up	Rolling	Down	Hard Down

17 LOS COYOTES INDIAN RESERVATION

ROUTE TYPE	Mixed Loop
DISTANCE	29.6 miles
RIDING TIME	4–5 Hours
ELEVATION GAIN	4500 ft
AEROBIC SCALE	5/5
BURN FACTOR	4/5
SCARE-O-METER	3/5
LAND MANAGER	Los Coyotes Indian Reservation
INFORMATION	760-782-2701

You can easily spend a full day exploring the physical challenges and aesthetic rewards of Los Coyotes Indian Reservation. Adjacent to the northwest corner of Anza-Borrego Desert State Park, the reservation offers pine forest, green valleys, desert vistas, steep mountain terrain, and, what you've all been waiting for, the highest point in San Diego County. At 6533 feet, Hot Springs Mountain shouldn't be missed. Getting there will cost you a few thousand calories, but you'll be glad you made the investment.

Los Coyotes Indian Reservation is one of the few parcels of "private" land where visitors (both motorized and non-motorized) are invited to enjoy the proprietary trails system. The reservation also maintains camping facilities for both day and overnight use. Encouraging limited public use generates a modest amount of supplemental income for the reservation. Entering the reservation, whether you are driving, walking, or biking, will cost you the relatively handsome sum of $10.00, but when you realize that those fees are securing access to an extensive trails system that would otherwise be completely off limits, it doesn't seem like much to pay. Although many miles of trail are open to visitors, there are some areas of the reservation that are closed to any public intrusion. You should think of the reservation as a private residence and stay out of any areas where you are not wanted. The reservation's hours of operation vary with the seasons and day of the week. Although generally open from morning to early evening on at least Fridays, Saturdays, and Sundays, you should definitely call ahead before making the long car trip.

Much of the ride outlined below puts you on occasionally steep and bumpy, but generally well-graded, dirt road. There is, however, an extensive network of narrow, ungraded, and unimproved roads where 4-wheel drive enthusiasts can often be found testing their machines against the laws of physics. You should expect to encounter vehicles on even the most remote trails.

THE DRIVE

Approach Warner Springs on Highway 79 from whatever direction is most convenient. Near the center of Warner Springs, at mile marker 35, you'll turn EAST on Camino San Ignacio. Bear RIGHT on Camino San Ignacio as it evolves into

Los Coyotes Indian Reservation—Ride 17

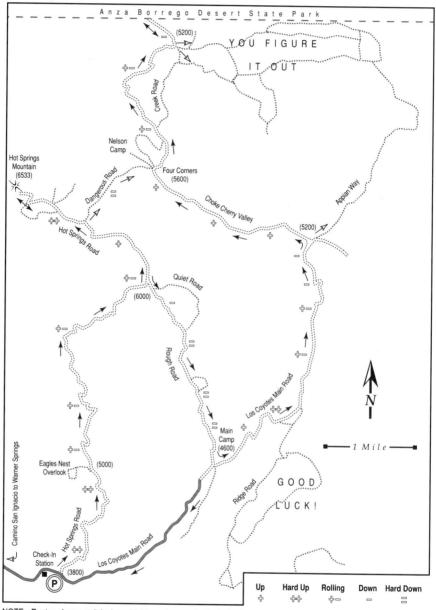

NOTE: Routes shown as "singletrack" (⋯⋯) are actually 4-wheel drive routes, and, in in most cases, can accomodate suitable motorized vehicles. All routes shown as "dirt roads" (⋯⋯), are relatively wide and well graded dirt roads.

Los Coyotes Road, heading southeast toward the reservation. In 4.5 miles you'll reach the entrance station to the reservation. Stop and pay whatever fees apply. You'll want to park near the entrance station so you may want to ask the attendant where you should leave the car.

RIDE 17

LOS COYOTES RESERVATION

INCREMENTAL DISTANCE	CUMULATIVE DISTANCE	DESCRIPTION OF RIDE	DISTANCE TO FINISH
	0.0	Start measuring from the entrance station. Continue up Los Coyotes Road into the reservation.	29.6
0.1	0.1	Turn LEFT onto Hot Springs Road and begin climbing.	29.5
	5.6	Pass Rough Road on your right.	24.0
	6.2	Pass Dangerous Road on your right.	23.4
7.7	7.8	Arrive at Hot Springs Peak. Check out the tower. Turn around and begin descending to Rough Road. Dangerous Road is also an excellent option that will get you to the other side of the reservation and shorten your day by several miles (see map).	21.8
2.4	10.2	Turn LEFT on Rough Road and soon descend toward the main camping area.	19.4
2.6	12.8	Arrive at the main camp area. Bear LEFT up the main road, passing the camping area on your left.	16.8
3.6	16.4	Bear LEFT at the fork heading up Choke Cherry Valley.	13.2
2.1	18.5	Arrive at Four Corners. Stay RIGHT to remain on the main road.	11.1
	20.9	Follow the road as it curves left.	8.7
2.7	21.2	This is the end of the reservation where it abuts state park property. Turn around and head back toward the reservation entrance or, if you're feeling fresh, explore the spider's web of 4-wheel drive routes east of your location.	8.4
8.4	29.6	Back at the car	0.0

Looking southwest from San Diego County's highest point—Hot Springs Mountain (6533').

Singletrack pioneers—every mountainbiker owes them a debt of gratitude

TRANSITIONAL AND
TRUE DESERT

18 McCAIN VALLEY

ROUTE TYPE	Out-n-Back
DISTANCE	27.8 miles
RIDING TIME	3-4 Hours
ELEVATION GAIN	1500 ft
AEROBIC SCALE	4/5
BURN FACTOR	2/5
SCARE-O-METER	2/5
LAND MANAGER	U.S. Department of Agriculture - Bureau of Land Management
INFORMATION	760-337-4400

The McCain Valley out-n-back is a lung-builder with a view. No map has been included for this easy to follow ride that stretches north-south in a nearly straight line across the dry, rolling chaparral on the northeastern edge of the In-Ko-Pah Mountains. Pretty darn hot in summer, the McCain Valley, like anything east of the Lagunas, is best visited during the cool season. The entire route is a very wide and well-graded sandy dirt road that can be enjoyed by novices looking for some backcountry experience as well as experts looking for a good workout. How hard you work is less a function of the road and more a matter of how fast you want to go.

Other than the sometimes bone-jarring washboard, there is no great technical challenge to this ride. Nevertheless, you'll definitely finish the day feeling like a mountain biker. For the more adventurous among you, it is certainly possible to leave the main road and explore some of the rideable, but often soft, singletrack trails that parallel the road in the brush. Just don't get too far from the main road and stay the heck off of any state park singletrack or designated wilderness. The McCain Valley Resource Conservation Area where you'll be riding is a BLM-managed land of many activities including hiking, biking, horseback riding, hunting, camping and off-highway vehicle riding. You may encounter motorized vehicles along the ride, so stay alert. Overnighting is definitely an option, and water is available at the camps. Contact the BLM for camping information.

THE DRIVE

I-8 east past Boulder Oaks and take the Highway 94/Campo/Boulevard exit. At the bottom of the ramp, Turn RIGHT (south) on Ribbonwood and continue 1.9 miles to Old Highway 80. Turn LEFT (east) and continue an additional 2.5 miles to McCain Valley Road. The measured ride begins here, although the first 2.3 miles of the ride will have you on pavement. If you prefer to drive in a bit further, just shorten the mileage below by the appropriate amount.

![RIDE 18]

McCAIN VALLEY

Incremental Distance	Cumulative Distance	Description of Ride	Distance to Finish
	0.0	Start from the intersection of Old Highway 80 and McCain Valley Road.	27.8
2.3	2.3	Dirt road begins at the cattle guard.	25.5
	2.6	Pass the turnoff to Sacatone Overlook on your Right. You may want to check it out later. The Carrizo Gorge is worth looking at.	25.2
	4.7	On your left, you'll be passing several entrances to the Lark Canyon OHV staging area.	23.1
	8.3	Pass the turnoff to the Carrizo Overlook on your right. Once again, check it out on the way back.	19.5
	12.3	Continue STRAIGHT past the Cottonwood camping area on both sides of the road.	15.5
11.6	13.9	Deadend. Turn around and head back the way you came in.	13.9
13.9	27.8	Back at the car.	0.0

19 JACUMBA MOUNTAINS

Table Mountain and Valley of the Moon, located in the extreme southeast corner of the county, offer a wonderful opportunity to experience the transitional zone where mountain chaparral begins to blend with the dry, prickly things reaching up from the desert of Imperial Valley. Don't put your foot (or any other body or bike part) down on any of the sharp, pointy stuff. Warm temperatures and well-drained, sandy soils make this an excellent cool season ride. Don't do it in summer. Both rides place you right along the eastern margin of the rocky and sometimes surreal looking Jacumba Mountains before they cross the border into Mexico. If you're looking for a bit of isolation, quirky rock formations (Valley of the Moon), great desert vistas, and a good workout, the combination of these two rides will leave you grinning. Although much of the area is open to motorized use, you are not likely to encounter much traffic, particularly north of I-8 in the Table Mountain area. Valley of the Moon is a bit more populated, so keep an eye out for 4-wheelers. As shown on the following map, you'll have to ditch your bike for the final stretch of the Valley of the Moon ride (19b) as it crosses into the Jacumba Mountains Wilderness (NO BIKES).

Table Mountain, Valley of the Moon—Rides 19a, 19b

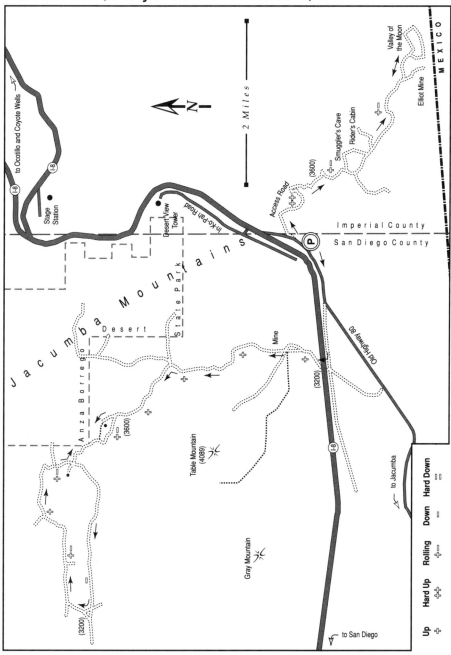

19a TABLE MOUNTAIN

ROUTE TYPE	Lollipop
DISTANCE	11.4
RIDING TIME	2.0 hours
ELEVATION GAIN	1000
AEROBIC SCALE	3/5
BURN FACTOR	2/5
SCARE-O-METER	2/5
LAND MANAGER	U.S. Department of Agriculture- Bureau of Land Management
INFORMATION	760-337-4400

Table Mountain looking southeast—if the heat doesn't get you, the cholla will.

The Table Mountain area just 5 minutes from Interstate 8.

This ride is fairly straight-forward and only partly desert-like, but you do need to keep in mind that it doesn't take long for one sandy wash to start looking just like the last one. The best way to avoid "desert déjà vu" is to take your time, don't get carried away, and always look around at the landmarks before turning on or off the trail. When in doubt, backtrack. You'll be heading around the backside of Table Mountain on the northeast side. There is also an option to climb Table Mountain itself, but you may want to wait until you've nearly finished the ride described below before throwing in the extra grunt to the peak. That option actually starts out near the beginning of the recommended ride. The peak will add about 600 feet of climbing and yet another vista to your day.

THE DRIVE

Take I-8 east approximately 70 miles from San Diego heading for the Imperial County line. Exit at In-Ko-Pah Park Road (last exit before the I-8 drops down to Ocotillo in Imperial Valley). Turn RIGHT at the bottom of the ramp and immediately RIGHT again onto Old Hwy 80. Proceed WEST approximately 0.25 miles to the unmarked but well-worn dirt turnout on the left. The measured ride starts here, but if you prefer to leave your vehicle out of sight of the highway, you can follow the dirt road leading east from the turnout toward Valley of the Moon (see map) and park in one of several smaller turnouts.

RIDE 19a

TABLE MOUNTAIN

Incremental Distance	Cumulative Distance	Description of Ride	Distance to Finish
	0.0	Start from the turnout on Old Hwy 80. Proceed west on the shoulder of Old Hwy 80.	11.4
0.7	0.7	Fork RIGHT off of Old Hwy 80 and onto the dirt frontage road. On your right you'll see a brake inspection area for vehicles traveling east on Hwy 8.	10.7
0.6	1.3	Turn RIGHT under Hwy 8.	10.1
	1.6	LEFT or RIGHT at the fork will get you to the same place.	9.8
	1.8	The two forks you encountered at 1.6 rejoin here. Continue STRAIGHT, remaining east of the drainage immediately on your left. If you look left across the drainage however, you'll see a road crossing the dry creekbed and seeming to head in the direction of the peak. Although it is a decent, short ride, it does NOT go to the peak but instead deadends at an old quarry now used as a shooting gallery. The old and faded access road to the peak actually starts out in the creekbed as well, just below the more obvious road to the quarry.	9.6 / 9.6
	2.1	Avoid the private property to your right.	9.3
1.8	3.1	Bear LEFT at the three-way fork. Anything else will take you on some lovely but mostly dead-end spurs.	8.3
	3.8	Bear RIGHT and take the brief but steep detour up to the antenna. It's worth the view.	7.6

		Take the singletrack down the backside to join the main road again.	
1.1	4.2	Bear LEFT at the locked gate. You'll be emerging from the road on the right in about an hour. Check your brakes because here comes the serious downhill of the day (Scare-o-meter 5). You will then continue straight down the sandy wash.	7.2
1.4	5.6	Turn RIGHT out of the wash and continue up past the rock piles and fire rings used by campers.	5.8
0.1	5.7	Continue to bear RIGHT heading back toward the ridge and antenna you left at 4.2.	5.7
0.3	6.0	Stay RIGHT again.	5.4
	6.4	Ignore the short deadend spur on your right.	5.0
0.7	6.7	Stay RIGHT again.	4.7
0.5	7.2	Finish the loop at the locked gate and head back the same way you came in.	4.2
4.2	11.4	Back at the car.	0.0

19b VALLEY OF THE MOON

ROUTE TYPE	Out-n-Back
DISTANCE	~7 miles
RIDING TIME	2.0 hours
ELEVATION GAIN	2000
AEROBIC SCALE	4/5
BURN FACTOR	5/5
SCARE-O-METER	4/5
LAND MANAGER	U.S. Department of Agriculture- Bureau of Land Management
INFORMATION	760-337-4400

Like the Table Mountain area, riding distances around Valley of the Moon will vary depending on how much exploring you do on the small network of hiking and 4-wheel drive truck routes. Once you've made the positively dizzying ascent straight up to the saddle, you should feel free to meander on past Smuggler's Cave and toward the Valley of the Moon area. Don't forget that you'll have to leave the bike behind before venturing onto any designated Wilderness (see the map). The international border is not always well marked so pay attention and STAY OUT OF MEXICO.

THE DRIVE

Follow the same driving and parking directions for Table Mountain above.

RIDE 19b

VALLEY OF THE MOON

INCREMENTAL DISTANCE	CUMULATIVE DISTANCE	DESCRIPTION OF RIDE	DISTANCE TO FINISH
	0.0	Start from the turnout on Old Hwy 80. Bear EAST then SOUTH on the dirt road leading from the turnout up to the saddle.	~7
1.5	1.5	Welcome to the saddle. Try to breathe. From this point on, simply make your way generally SOUTH toward the international border along any of the several 4-wheel drive routes.	~5.5
~2.0	~3.5	Turn around when you've seen enough. Don't crash on the downhill.	~3.5
~3.5	~7	Back at the car.	0.0

20 ANZA-BORREGO DESERT

San Diego County's deserts are not to be missed. The eastern part of our region is defined by a magnificent and rugged wilderness that few people visit more than perhaps once a year, typically in the springtime to see the famous bloom of our fickle local cacti. If you haven't had the time to explore the seemingly endless hiking and biking opportunities that await you, you may want to think about rearranging your schedule and stocking up on sunscreen.

Fortunately, a large portion of the desert region enjoys protected status as part of Anza-Borrego Desert State Park. The only bad news is the fact that current state park policy excludes mountain bikes from all but the approximately 500 miles of paved and dirt road within the park. Even so, there are obviously many miles of challenging riding that could easily occupy you for many months, preferably in the dead of winter. The two rides outlined below are merely an introduction to the myriad routes you may want to explore. From Coyote Canyon to the Badlands to Pinyon and Split Mountains, you should never again think of the Anza-Borrego Desert region as merely a place to view wildflowers from the front seat of your car.

I have recommended two fairly long routes that you should feel free to shorten in accordance with your fitness level and the day's expected high temperature. It goes without saying that you'll be steering clear of the desert during

3 Canyons—Rodriguez/Oriflamme/Chariot—Ride 20a

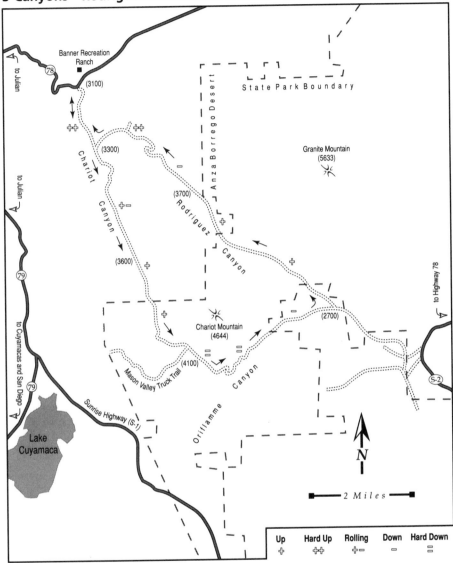

the summer, but you need to expect that you can easily roast in winter as well. There's no avoiding the fact that the desert can present you with a lot of sandy riding, but I hope you'll find that the rides listed below don't put you in the deep stuff very often.

20a THREE CANYONS— RODRIGUEZ/ORIFLAMME/CHARIOT

ROUTE TYPE	Loop
DISTANCE	16.1
RIDING TIME	4 Hours
ELEVATION GAIN	2600
AEROBIC SCALE	5/5
BURN FACTOR	4/5
SCARE-O-METER	3/5
LAND MANAGER	Anza-Borrego Desert State Park
	U.S. Department of Agriculture- Bureau of Land Management
INFORMATION	760-767-4684 or 760-767-4205 (State Parks)
	760-337-4400 (BLM)

In case you thought the desert was flat, here's a wake-up call. The three canyons you'll be exploring on this ride will take you from transitional chaparral to true desert. The first third of this ride is the relatively "wet" part as you cling to the edge of the Laguna Mountains rising to the west. But by mile 6 you'll be checking your water supply, energy level, and brake pads as Oriflamme Canyon opens up beneath you and beckons you east into the dryness below. The hair-raising descent to the bottom of Oriflamme will eventually place you into Rodriguez Canyon for the thankfully more gradual climb back to the start of the ride.

THE DRIVE

From Julian, take Highway 78 (Banner Road) east 6.6 miles down Banner Canyon toward the desert. Look for the Chariot Canyon access road on your right just before mile marker 65.0 and the Banner Recreation Ranch entrance on your left. Look for parking. The ride starts from Highway 78 heading southeast on the dirt of Chariot Canyon Road.

RIDE 20a

THREE CANYONS— RODRIGUEZ/ORIFLAMME/CHARIOT

INCREMENTAL DISTANCE	CUMULATIVE DISTANCE	DESCRIPTION OF RIDE	DISTANCE TO FINISH
	0.0	Start climbing southeast on Chariot Canyon Road from its intersection with Highway 78.	16.1
1.4		Pass Rodriguez Canyon Road on your left. You'll be emerging from there in 3 to 4 hours.	14.7

	1.7	Continue STRAIGHT past the turnoff on your right.	14.4
	2.1	Arrive at the saddle and begin descending. You may encounter "Private Property" signs but you may continue as long as you stay on the road.	14.0
4.3	4.3	Pass the Mason Valley Truck Trail turnoff on your right. You will now descend sharply into Oriflamme Canyon.	11.8
	7.9	BEWARE. You may encounter a wire fence across the road. Open and close it behind you.	8.2
4.8	9.1	Take a hard LEFT onto Rodriguez Canyon Road as is climbs gradually northwest. Granite Mountain is on your right.	7.0
	12.8	Arrive at the saddle, continue straight and begin descending. Stay on the main road as it eventually climbs back up to rejoin Chariot Canyon.	3.3
5.6	14.7	Turn RIGHT on Chariot Canyon Road and return to Highway 78 the way you came in.	1.4
1.4	16.1	Back at the car.	0.0

20b GRAPEVINE CANYON

ROUTE TYPE	Lollipop
DISTANCE	30.5 miles
RIDING TIME	5-6 hours
ELEVATION GAIN	2700
AEROBIC SCALE	5/5
BURN FACTOR	4/5
Scare-o-meter	3/5
LAND MANAGER	Anza-Borrego Desert State Park and County of San Diego
INFORMATION	760-767-4684 or 760-767-4205 (State Parks)

You'll get a suntan, a workout, and a serious downhill on this long and delicious lollipop. Big elevation changes ensure quite a bit of ecological diversity as you rise and fall along the western edge of Anza-Borrego State Park. The many "No Trespassing" signs that you will encounter along this ride are intended to keep visitors off of the private property adjacent to the public road easement. The recommended ride starts from the Yaqui Well/Tamarisk Grove area of the State Park, but you can certainly modify or shorten the ride by starting from approximately the halfway point, somewhere along S-22 in Ranchita. Beware, however, because you'll simply be putting off quite a bit of climbing until the end of the ride when you will NOT be feeling your freshest.

Grapevine Canyon—Ride 20b

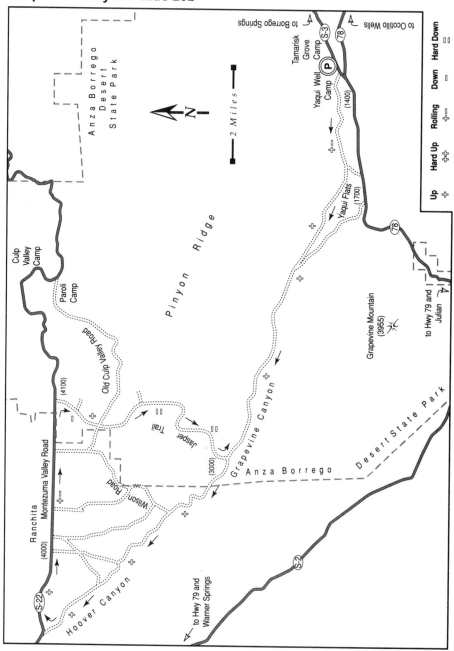

THE DRIVE

The recommended ride starts from the Yaqui Well turnoff approximately 10 miles south of Borrego Springs, off of Road S-3, just north of its intersection with Highway 78. If you're coming down Highway 78 from Julian, you'll just continue east passing through Scissors Crossing and eventually turning LEFT (north) on S-3 before parking at Yaqui Well or Tamarisk Grove.

RIDE 20b

GRAPEVINE CANYON

Incremental Distance	Cumulative Distance	Description of Ride	Distance to Finish
	0.0	Start measuring from the intersection of Grapevine Canyon Road (Yaqui Well Camp) and S-3 where it meets Highway 78. Head west on Grapevine Canyon Road.	30.5
	0.5	Pass the turnoff to Yaqui Well on your right.	30.0
	2.1	Stay STRAIGHT, passing the turnoff to Plum Canyon and Highway 78 on your left.	28.4
	4.1	STRAIGHT past the second Plum Canyon/Highway 78 turnoff on your left.	26.4
	8.2	Make note of the Jasper Trail on your right. You'll be emerging from there in a couple of hours. Continue to climb on Grapevine Canyon Road. You'll soon exit ABDSP at mile 8.6.	22.3
9.0	9.0	Bear RIGHT at the split.	21.5
1.1	10.1	Bear LEFT to continue up Grapevine Canyon. Right turn option will take you back to Ranchita via Wilson Road.	20.4
	10.5	STRAIGHT past the turnoff on your right.	20.0
	11.5	STRAIGHT past the turnoff on your right.	19.0
	11.6	Bear RIGHT to remain on Grapevine Canyon.	18.9
2.4	12.5	Arrive at S-22 (Montezuma Valley Road). Turn RIGHT onto the pavement and head east toward Ranchita.	18.0
4.3	16.8	Turn RIGHT onto the dirt of Jasper Trail just before mile marker 7.0. The trail will roll for a couple of miles before descending sharply.	13.7
	17.4	Ignore the spur on your left.	13.1
1.4	18.2	CROSS Culp Valley Road.	12.3
4.1	22.3	Turn LEFT onto Grapevine Canyon Road. It should look familiar.	8.2
8.2	30.5	Back at the car.	0.0

APPENDIX
KEY CONTACTS

Anza-Borrego Desert State Park
P.O. Box 299
Borrego Springs, CA 92004
Phone: 760-767-4205 (visitor center), 619-767-5311 (administration)

City of Escondido - Dept. of Public Works - Parks, Lakes and Open Space Div.
475 North Spruce Street
Escondido, CA 92025
Phone: 760-741-4668

City of Poway - Public Services Department - Trails Division
P.O. Box 789
Poway, CA 92074
Phone: 619-679-5423

City of San Diego - Department of Parks and Recreation
City Administration Building, 9th Floor
202 C Street
San Diego, CA 92101
Phone: Coastal 619-221-8906
        Inland 619-685-1300
        Metro 619-235-1120
        Northern 619-525-8222

Cleveland National Forest - Descanso Ranger District
3348 Alpine Blvd.
Alpine, CA 91901
Phone: 619-445-6235
Fax: 619-445-1753

Cleveland National Forest - Palomar Ranger District
1634 Black Canyon Road
Ramona, CA 92065
Phone: 760-788-0250
Fax: 619-788-6130

Cuyamaca Rancho State Park
12551 Highway 79
Descanso, CA 92016
Phone: 760-765-0755

International Mountain Bicycling Association (IMBA)
P.O. Box 7578
Boulder, CO 80306-7578

Phone: 303-545-9011
Fax: 303-545-9026
http://www.outdoorlink.com/IMBA/

Laguna Mountain Volunteer Association (LMVA)
c/o Cleveland National Forest - Descanso Ranger District
3348 Alpine Blvd.
Alpine, CA 91901
Phone: 619-445-6235
Fax: 619-445-1753

Olivenhain Municipal Water District
1966 Olivenhain Road
Encinitas, CA 92024
Phone: 760-753-6466

Palomar Mountain State Park
P.O. Box 175
Palomar Mountain, CA 92060
Phone: 760-742-3462 or 760-765-0755

San Diego Audubon Society
2321 Morena Blvd., Suite D
San Diego, CA 92110
Phone: 619-275-0557

San Diego County Department of Parks and Recreation
5201 Ruffin Road
San Diego, CA 92123
Phone: 619-565-3600

San Diego County Trails Council, Inc.
P. O. Box 2727
El Cajon, CA 92021-0727
Phone: 619-563-5025
Fax: 619-561-7755

San Diego Mountain Biking Association (SDMBA)
P.O. Box 881491
San Diego, CA 92168-1491
Phone: 619-258-9140
http://www2.connectnet.com/~taffe/cycle/SDMBA/SDMBA.html

San Dieguito River Park - Joint Powers Authority
1500 State Street, Suite 280
San Diego, CA 92101
Phone: 619-235-5440

Sierra Club, San Diego Chapter
3820 Ray Street

San Diego, CA 92104
Phone: 619-299-1743

Sweetwater Authority
P.O. Box 2328
Chula Vista, CA 91912-2328
Phone: 619-420-1413 ext. 102

U.S. Bureau of Land Management
1661 South 4th Street
El Centro, CA 92243
760-337-4400

U. S. Department of the Interior - Fish and Wildlife Service
2736 Loker Avenue, West, Suite A
Carlsbad, CA 92008
Phone: 760-930-0168

Scott Owen of the San Diego Mountain Biking Association busily representing the interests of riders like you and me.

RECOMMENDED READING

The following books and maps are in print (1997) and are available at major book-stores in Southern California. Contact Sunbelt Publications, telephone (619) 258-4911, for more information. These titles are recommended to enhance the understanding and enjoyment of cycling in the San Diego region.

ADVENTURING IN THE CALIFORNIA DESERT   Foster   0-87156-721-0
Best single reference to the natural history and destinations in the local deserts including walks and drives in Anza-Borrego, Yuha Desert, and Salton Sea area.

AFOOT AND AFIELD IN SAN DIEGO COUNTY, 3rd Ed.   Schad   0-89997-158-X
The best-selling guide to San Diego outdoors. 192 hikes are described, many are appropriate for mountain biking. Excellent maps, photos, and appendix.

ANZA-BORREGO DESERT REGION, 3rd Ed.   Lindsay   0-89997-129-6
Latest updates to the comprehensive guide to Southern California's most popular desert playground. Includes detailed map (also available separately). Details of dozens of dirt roads open to mountain bikes.

BASIC ESSENTIALS MOUNTAIN BIKING   Strassman   0-934802-47-5
One of the "Basic Essentials" series, this book covers all levels of mountain biking, from novice to pro. Safety and maintenance are also reviewed.

BICYCLE REPAIR BOOK   Van der Plas   0-933201-55-9
A thorough review of bicycle maintenance, repair, and troubleshooting, covering everything from simple frame straightening to installing bicycle lights. Also useful is the guide to home-made tools and repair equipment.

BICYCLE RIDES SAN DIEGO   Brundige   0-9619151-4-5
Description of bicycling trips through the valleys, canyons and mountains of San Diego County include detailed maps, difficulty, distance, and highlights.

BICYCLING THE PACIFIC COAST   Kirkendall   0-89886-232-9
A detailed guidebook to the Pacific Coast bicycle route, which stretches from Mexico to Canada through California, Oregon and Washington. The 1,947 mile route is broken down into 50 mile-segments.

CALIFORNIA OHV GUIDEBOOK   Llewellyn   0-941925-10-2
Complete guidebook to off-highway vehicular recreation in California. Includes maps and other information about OHV areas and "green sticker roads." With index and locator maps, this book is both highly informative and easy to use - a "must" for every OHV enthusiast who wants to go adventuring beyond the pavement's end. Many trails suitable for mountain biking.

CUYAMACA RANCHO STATE PARK HIKE MAP   Harrison   1-877689-37-8
A detailed map of Cuyamaca Rancho State Park showing campgrounds, hiking and horseback riding trails, and topography. Mountain bike routes are clearly delineated.

CYCLING SAN DIEGO, 2nd Ed.   Schad   0-961728-83-3
Newly revised, comprehensive guide to 60 day trips in San Diego County ranging from leisurely rides to more difficult routes including cultural and natural features.

MOUNTAIN BICYCLING SAN GABRIELS   Immler   0-89997-078-8
Includes over 30 tours in the Los Angeles National Forest, ranging in length from 2 to 35 miles, and varying in difficulty from easy to rides up mountain peaks. Distance and elevation gain are included with each description.

MOUNTAIN BIKING AROUND LOS ANGELES   Immler   0-89997-109-1
Listed are 32 mountain bicycling trips in the grater Los Angeles area, form Malibu to Orange County. Total distance, difficult, elevation gain or loss, time to complete the trip, and a map is included for each trip.

MOUNTAIN BIKING SOUTHERN CALIFORNIA'S BEST 100 TRAILS   Douglass and Fragnoli   0-938665-20-0
All the best places to ride a mountain bike--from San Diego to San Luis Obispo, from the Sierra Nevada to Death Valley and the Mojave Desert--the west's leading mountain biking authors share their top choices of fat-tired routes.

SAN DIEGO: INTRODUCTION TO REGION 3rd Ed.   Pryde   0-8403-3233-5
The reference to the natural environments of the county. Includes: Geology, Climate, Soils, Vegetation, Wildlife, Water Supply (most important!).

SAN DIEGO COUNTY, AAA GUIDEBOOK
From Mission Bay to Borrego Springs, from Coronado to Lake Cuyamaca, San Diego County encompasses beaches, canyons, mountains and desert. This latest Auto Club 300-plus-page San Diego County guidebook contains more than 140 photographs and 30 maps, all in full color.

SIDEKICK MAP-SMUGGLER'S CAVE   Sidekick   1-880824-16-7
Located 65 miles east of San Diego off Highway 8 near the town of Jacumba. Explore a cave used by smugglers in the 1800's, a section of the Butterfield Overland Stage route or enjoy the vistas of the old railroad.

WEEKENDERS GUIDE: ANZA-BORREGO 2nd Ed.   Johnson   0-910805-05-9
Rides along paved and dirt desert roads with all-color photos by a veteran Anza-Borrego naturalist and professional photographer. Detailed maps supplement descriptions with post mile markers carefully locating points of interest.

INDEX

A

Agua Tibia Wilderness (Palomar Mountain), 79
Al Bahr Shrine Camp (Laguna Mountains), 52
Alpine Blvd (Alpine), 47, 49
Anderson Road (Alpine), 49
Anderson Truck Trail (Cleveland National Forest), 47
Anza-Borrego Desert State Park, 83, 96
Arroyo Seco Trail (Cuyamaca Rancho State Park), 66, 71
Avenida La Valencia (Poway), 32
Azalea Glen Loop Trail (Cuyamaca Rancho State Park), 66, 71
Azalea Spring (Cuyamaca Rancho State Park), 66, 71

B

Badlands (Anza-Borrego Desert), 96
Balboa Ave, 8
Balboa Park, 11
Banner Canyon (Anza-Borrego Desert), 98
Banner Recreation Ranch (Anza-Borrego Desert), 98
Banner Road (Anza-Borrego Desert), 98
Barker Canyon (Palomar Mountain), 79
Barker Spur Trail (Palomar Mountain), 79
Barker Way (Mission Trails Regional Park), 14, 15, 16
best expert rides, xxvii
best intermediate rides, xxvii
best novice rides, xxvii
Big Laguna Lake (Laguna Mountains), 52
Big Laguna Trail (Laguna Mountains), xxvii, 50, 52
Biltmore Trail (Marian Bear Memorial Park), 2
Black Mountain Road, 10, 11
Blood Hill (Mission Trails Regional Park), 20, 21
Mission Trails Regional Park, 20
Blue Sky Ecological Reserve (Poway), 31
Bobcat Meadow (Corral Canyon), 74
Bonita Road, 44
Borrego Springs, 101
Boucher Lookout Loop (Palomar Mountain), 77
Boulder Creek (Cuyamaca Mountains), 68, 70
Boulder Creek Road (Cuyamaca Mountains), 70

Boulder Loop Trail (Daley Ranch), 36
Boulder Oaks (McCain Valley), 89
Bronco Flats (Corral Canyon), 75
Buckman Springs (Laguna Mountains), 57, 58, 60, 74
Burnt Mountain (Daley Ranch), 36

C

Cactus Hill (Sweetwater Reservoir), 44
California Riding and Hiking Trail (Cuyamaca Rancho State Park), 66, 71
Calle De Vida (Tierrasanta), 18, 19, 21
Camino San Ignacio (Los Coyotes Indian Reservation), 83
Campo Road (Bonita), 43
Canyonside Community Park (Los Penasquitos Canyon Preserve), 11
Carrizo Overlook (Anza-Borrego Desert), 90
Carson Crossing (Los Penasquitos Canyon), 10
Central Valley Loop Trail (Daley Ranch), 36
Champagne Pass (Laguna Mountains), 55
Chaparral Loop Trail (Daley Ranch), 36
Chariot Canyon Road (Anza-Borrego Desert), 98, 99
Chariot Canyon (Anza-Borrego Desert), 98
Chihuahua Valley Road, 81
Choke Cherry Valley (Los Coyotes Indian Reservation), 85
Church of Singletrack Consciousness, xiii
Cibbets Flat Camp (Laguna Mountains), 60
Clairemont Drive, 8
Clairemont Mesa Blvd, 2, 5, 7
Cold Stream Trail (Cuyamaca Rancho State Park), 65
Colina Dorada (Tierrasanta), 18
Conejos Trail (Cuyamaca Rancho State Park), 66, 71
Corral Canyon, 57, 72, 73, 74, 75
Corral Canyon Road, 74, 75
Cottonwood camping area (McCain Valley), 90
Cowles Mountain (Mission Trails Regional Park), xxii, 13, 14, 15, 16
Coyote Canyon (Anza-Borrego Desert), 96

Cutca Trail (Palomar Mountain), 79
Cuyamaca Peak (Cuyamaca Rancho State Park), 68, 70
Cuyamaca Rancho State Park, xv, xxvii, 61, 63, 68

D

Daley Ranch, xxvii, 34, 36
Dangerous Road (Los Coyotes Indian Reservation), 85
Deer Park Road (Laguna Mountains), 63
Del Dios Highway, 23
Del Poniente Trail (Poway), 30, 32
Descanso, 71
Dixon Lake (Escondido), 34, 36
downhilling, xxi

E

E Street/Bonita Road, 44
East Mesa Fire Road (Cuyamaca Rancho State Park), 63, 67, 68, 72
East Side Trail (Cuyamaca Rancho State Park), 63, 71, 72
El Capitan Reservoir, 47, 49
El Norte Parkway, 34
Elfin Forest, xiii, xxvii, 37, 38, 39
Engelmann Oak Loop Trail (Daley Ranch), 36
Engineers Road (Cleveland National Forest), 70
Equine Incline (Elfin Forest), 40
Escondido Creek (Elfin Forest), 37
Espola Road (Poway), 31, 32

F

Father Junipero Serra Trail (Mission Trails Regional Park), xiii, 13, 14, 15, 16, 19, 20
Felicita Creek (Lake Hodges), 25
Fern Flat (Cuyamaca Rancho State Park), 66, 71
First Aid, xx
Florida Canyon, 11
Florida Street, 11
Fortuna Mountain (Mission Trails Regional Park), 18, 19, 20, 21
Four Corners (Mission Trails Regional Park), 18, 19, 21
Four Corners (Corral Canyon), 74, 75, 85
Fred Canyon Road (Laguna Mountains), 59, 61

G

Garden Road, 28
Genesee Avenue, 2
Golden Triangle, 8
Golfcrest Drive, 16

Goodan Ranch, 26, 28
Granite Mountain (Anza-Borrego Desert), 99
Grapevine Canyon (Anza-Borrego Desert), xxiv, 99, 101
Grapevine Canyon Road (Anza-Borrego Desert), 101
Green Valley Fire Road (Cuyamaca Rancho State Park), 63, 65
Gun Slinger (Corral Canyon), 75

H
Hale, 38
Halfway Truck Trail (Palomar Mountain), 79
Harbison Canyon Road (Alpine), 47
Harbison Canyon/Dunbar Lane (Alpine), 47
Harmony Grove Road, 38, 39
Harvey Moore Trail (Cuyamaca Rancho State Park), 65, 71
Hernandez Hideaway (Lake Hodges), 26
High Point Truck Trail (Palomar Mountain), 78, 79
Highway 76, 77
Highway 78, 98, 99, 101
Holidays On Horseback, 70
Hoover Canyon (Anza-Borrego Desert), 101
Horse Canyon (Laguna Mountains), 58
Hot Springs Mountain (Los Coyotes Indian Reservation), xxvii, 83
Hot Springs Road (Los Coyotes Indian Reservation), 85
Hual-Cu-Cuish Camp (Cuyamaca Rancho State Park), 65, 71

I
Imperial Valley, 90, 94
Indian Creek (Laguna Mountains), 53, 55
Indian Creek Trail (Laguna Mountains), 55
Indian Flats, 80, 81
In-Ko-Pah Mountains, 89
In-Ko-Pah Park Road, 94
International Mountain Bicycling Association, ix, xvi

J
Jacaranda Place, 11
Jackson Drive, 14
Jacumba Mountains, 90
Japacha Fire Road (Cuyamaca Rancho State Park), 66, 71
Jasper Trail (Anza-Borrego Desert), 101
Julian, 23, 63, 70, 98, 101

K
Kearnan Cycle Trail (Corral Canyon), 73, 74, 75

Kitchen Creek (Laguna Mountains), 59
Kitchen Creek Road (Laguna Mountains), 57, 60
Kumeyaay Indians, xiii
Kwaay Pay (Mission Trails Regional Park), 13

L
La Cima Conservation Camp, 65
La Honda Drive, 34
La Mesa, 13
La Posta Road (Laguna Mountains), 59, 60, 61
La Posta Truck Trail (Laguna Mountains), 60, 61
Laguna Camp (Laguna Mountains), 52
Laguna Meadow (Laguna Mountains), 52, 55
Laguna Meadow Road (Laguna Mountains), 55
Laguna Recreation Area, 52
Lake Cuyamaca, 71
Lake Drive (Lake Hodges), 25
Lake Hodges, xxvii, 22, 23, 26, 41
Lake Morena, 72, 74
Lake Poway, 29, 30, 31, 32
Lake Poway Road, 31
Lakeview Ridge Trail (Elfin Forest), 37, 41
Lark Canyon OHV staging area (McCain Valley), 90
Lookout Road (Cuyamaca Rancho State Park), 66, 71
Lopez Canyon (Los Penasquitos Canyon Preserve), 10, 11
Los Coyotes Indian Reservation, xxvii, 83
Los Coyotes Road, 85
Los Penasquitos Canyon Preserve, 8, 10
Los Penasquitos Creek, 10
Los Vaqueros Horse Camp (Cuyamaca Rancho State Park) (65
Los Vaqueros Road (Cuyamaca Rancho State Park), 65
Lost Valley Road (Indian Flats), 81

M
Marian Bear, 1
Marian Bear Memorial Park, 1
Marian Bear Park, 2, 4, 5
Martha's Grove (Sycamore Canyon), 26, 29
Mason Canyon Road (Anza-Borrego Desert), 99
McCain Valley, 89
McCain Valley Road, xxvii, 89, 90
Merigan Fire Road (Cuyamaca Rancho State Park), 70, 72
Merigan Ranch, 70
Mesa Drive, 15

Middle Peak (Cuyamaca Rancho State Park), 65, 71
Midland Road, 32
Milk Ranch Road (Cuyamaca Rancho State Park), 65, 71
Mission Bay, 7
Mission Gorge Road, 13, 14, 15, 16, 19
Mission San Diego de Alcala, 13
Mission Trails Regional Park, 13
Montezuma Valley Road (Anza-Borrego Desert), 101
Morena Stokes Valley Road (Corral Canyon), 74
Morley Field Drive, 11
Mormon Battalion, xiii
Mount Israel (Elfin Forest), 37
mountain lions, xix
Mt. Acadia Avenue, 8
Mt. Woodson (Poway), 30, 31

N
9th Avenue/Auto Parkway, 38
Nate Harrison Grade (Palomar Mountain), 75, 77, 78
Nate Harrison Road (Palomar Mountain), 77
Noble Canyon (Laguna Mountains), xxvii, 52, 53, 54, 55
Noble Canyon Trail (Laguna Mountains), 52, 53, 56
North Clairemont Recreation Center (Tecolote Canyon), 8
North Fortuna Peak (Mission Trails Regional Park), 13, 20
North Peak (Cuyamaca Rancho State Park), 70
North Point Loop (Elfin Forest), 40
Northshore Primitive Camping Area (Lake Morena), 74

O
Oak Canyon (Mission Trails Regional Park), 20, 21
Oak Grove Truck Trail (Palomar Mountain), 78
Oak Grove Drive, 70
Oak Grove Truck Trail (Palomar Mountain), 79
Oak Valley (Elfin Forest), 37, 41
Oakzanita Peak (Cuyamaca Rancho State Park), 66, 67, 68
Oakzanita Trail (Cuyamaca Rancho State Park), 63
Old Highway 80, 54, 60, 61, 89, 90, 94, 96
Old Mission Dam Historic Area (Mission Trails Regional Park), 13, 20
Oriflamme Canyon (Anza-Borrego Desert), 98

P
Pacific Crest Trail, 15, 60, 61
Palomar Divide Truck Trail (Palomar Mountain), 78, 79

Palomar Mountain, 75
Palomar Mountain State Park, 77
Pauma Valley, 75
Pebble Beach Drive, 28
Peutz Valley Road (Alpine), 47, 49
Piedras Pintadas Trail (Lake Hodges), 25
Pine Creek Road (Laguna Mountains), 54, 55, 56
Pine Valley, 52, 54, 60
Pinyon Mountain (Anza-Borrego Desert), 96
Pioneer Mail (Laguna Mountains), 55
Plum Canyon (Anza-Borrego Desert), 101
poison oak, xx
Pomerado Road, 32
Poway, 26, 28, 29, 30
Poway Road, 28
Pyles Peak (Mission Trails Regional Park), 13

Q
Quail Trail (Elfin Forest), 40, 41
Questhaven Road, 39

R
Ranch House Loop Trail (Daley Ranch), 36
Ranch Road, 101
Ranchita, 101
Rancho Fanita Drive, 15
Rancho San Diego, 43
Rancho Santa Fe Road, 39
rattlesnake, xviii
Regents Road, 2, 5
Ribbonwood, 89
Ride Recommendations by Skill Level, xxvi
Riding With Children, xxii
Rim Trail (Mission Trail Regional Park), 21
Riverside Drive, 70
Rodriguez Canyon (Anza-Borrego Desert), 98, 99
Rose Canyon Open Space Park, 2, 4, 5
Rough Road (Los Coyotes Indian Reservation), 85
Rules of the Trail - IMBA, xvii

S
Sacatone Overlook (Anza-Borrego Desert), 90
Saddle Up Trail (Elfin Forest), 41
San Clemente Canyon, 1, 4, 5

San Diego County Trails Council, ix, xvi
San Diego Mountain Biking Association, ix, xvi, xxii, xxiv, 10
San Diego River, 13, 18, 19, 21
San Dieguito Marsh, 23
San Dieguito River, 22, 23
San Miguel Road, 44
sand, riding tips, xxii
Santee, 13, 15, 26, 28
Santee Lakes, 28
Scissors Crossing, 101
Sheephead Mountain Road (Laguna Mountains), 57, 60
Skye Valley Road (Corral Canyon), 75
Smuggler's Cave (Valley of the Moon), 95
Snead Avenue, 8
Soapstone Grade Road (Cuyamaca Rancho State Park), 65
Sorrento Valley Blvd, 10
Sorrento Valley Road, 10
South Fortuna Mountain (Mission Trails Regional Park), 13, 21
Split Mountain (Anza-Borrego Desert), 96
Standley Trail (Marian Bear Memorial Park), 2
Stonewall Peak (Cuyamaca Rancho State Park), 65
Summer Sage Road, 32
Summit Meadow Road, 44
Sunrise Highway (Laguna Mountains), 52, 53, 55, 57, 59, 60
Sunset Drive, 25
Sunset Trail (Laguna Mountains), 52
Suycott Wash (Mission Trails Regional Park), xxiv, 18, 19, 20, 21
Sweetwater Park Summit Site (Sweetwater Reservoir), 43
Sweetwater Reservoir, xxvii, 41
Sweetwater River, 43, 63, 65
Sweetwater Staging Area (Cuyamaca Rancho State Park), 71
switchbacks, xxi
Sycamore Canyon Open Space Preserve, xxvii, 26, 28
Sycamore Park Drive, 28, 29

T
Table Mountain, xxiv, xxvii, 90, 92, 93, 95
Tamarisk Grove (Anza-Borrego Desert), 99
Tecolote Canyon Golf Course, 7
Tecolote Canyon Natural Park, 7
Tecolote Road, 7
Ted Williams Parkway, 31
Temecula Creek, 79
Thing Ranch Road (Laguna Mountains), 61
Thing Valley (Laguna Mountains), xxvii, 59, 60
Thing Valley Road (Laguna Mountains), 59
Tierrasanta, 13, 18, 19
Tri-Canyons, 1
Twin Peaks (Poway), 29, 31, 32
Twin Peaks Road, 31
Tyke's Hike (Elfin Forest), 40

U
University City High School, 5
uphilling, xxi

V
Valley of the Moon, 90, 94, 95
Valley View Ledge Trail (Elfin Forest), 41
Via Rancho Parkway, 25
Victoria Drive, 49
Viejas Grade, 70
Visitor Center Loop Trail (Mission Trails Regional Park), 19
Volcan Mountain, 23

W
Warner Springs, 78, 81, 83
waterbars, xxii
Way Up Trail (Elfin Forest), 40, 41
West Bernardo Drive, 25
West Fortuna Trail (Mission Trails Regional Park), 19
West Mesa Trail (Cuyamaca Rancho State Park), 66, 71
West Side Trail (Cuyamaca Rancho State Park), 66, 71
Wilhelm Wolf, xiii
Wrangler (Corral Canyon, 74

Y
Yaqui Well (Anza-Borrego Desert), 99, 101

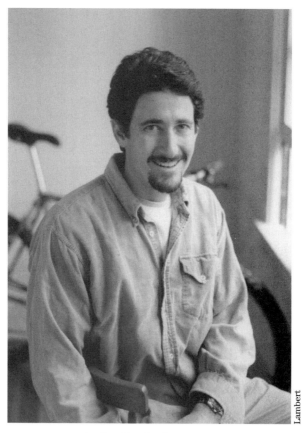

Author Daniel Greenstadt

With the purchase of his first fat tire bicycle in 1984, Daniel Greenstadt began a love affair with off-road cycling that has led him along trails and pathways throughout the United States and abroad. Since arriving in San Diego County in 1989, Daniel has been exploring the region's backcountry trails by bicycle, by foot, and, occasionally, on horseback. Daniel's commitment to the acquisition and preservation of trails for bicycling, hiking and equestrian use has led to his involvement with national and local trail advocacy groups including the San Diego County Trails Council and the San Diego Mountain Biking Association.

Daniel holds an undergraduate degree in Asian Studies from the University of California Santa Barbara and a Master of Pacific International Affairs from the Graduate School of International Relations and Pacific Studies at the University of California San Diego. Daniel is an expert on domestic and international markets for environmental goods and services, and currently consults on these and related economic and business matters for public and private sector clients. Daniel is also an avid cook, part-time graphic designer and a world traveler.

Help! We Need Your Comments

Every guidebook has its imperfections, and we'd like you to point them out. If you have any questions or comments that you feel might improve future editions of the San Diego Mountain Bike Guide, please take a few minutes to fill out the form below. We're counting on you to complain as much as possible. Thanks.

How did you acquire your copy of the San Diego Mountain Bike Guide?
___ Book Store   ___ Bike Shop   ___ Outdoor Retailer   ___ Gift

What do you find most useful about the book? _____

_____

_____

What do you find least useful about the book? _____

_____

_____

Would you recommend the book to a friend?   ___ Yes   ___ No

Do you look forward to future editions and updates?   ___ Yes   ___ No

Other comments: _____

_____

_____

If you'd like to receive additional information about mountain biking opportunities in the San Diego region and other Sunbelt publications, please complete the following:

Name:_____

Address:_____ Zip:_____

Phone/Fax/Email:_____

Mail or fax to:

Sunbelt Publications
1250 Fayette Street
El Cajon, CA 92020-1511
Fax: 619-258-4916